Be a Birder

Be a Birder

Best wishes

Hamza Yassin

Be a Birder

The Joy of Birdwatching and How to Get Started

HAMZA YASSIN

First published in Great Britain in 2023 by Gaia,
an imprint of Octopus Publishing Group Ltd
Carmelite House
50 Victoria Embankment
London EC4Y 0DZ
www.octopusbooks.co.uk

An Hachette UK Company
www.hachette.co.uk

ISBN 978-1-85675-509-2

A CIP catalogue record for this book is available from the British Library.

Printed and bound in the UK.

Typeset in 11.75/18pt Avenir by Jouve (UK), Milton Keynes.

3 5 7 9 10 8 6 4 2

Commissioning Editor: Nicola Crane
Design Director: Mel Four
Senior Editor: Leanne Bryan
Copy Editor: Vimbai Shire
Illustrator: Rebecca Seddon
Assistant Production Manager: Allison Gonsalves

This FSC® label means that materials used
for the product have been responsibly sourced.

*To my family, and to my second family
and community in Ardnamurchan.*

CONTENTS

INTRODUCTION

I absolutely love birds. They make me tick. It's no exaggeration to say that I wake up and go to sleep thinking about birds. All of my conversations get redirected back to birds somehow.

And I'm so lucky to have a career that used to be my hobby. That's all thanks to birds.

Birds have been with me my entire life – from the colourful Weaver Birds on the banks of the Nile in Sudan to the Magpies of Newcastle. From the roosting Peregrine Falcons on the Carlsberg Brewery sign near my parents' house in Northampton to the White-tailed Eagles that I can see from the living-room window in Ardnamurchan, on the west coast of Scotland. Pretty much wherever you are in the world, you're going to find a bird.

I was in the Canadian Arctic in 2021 and there was nothing but ice and snow for as far as you could see.

No sign of trees at all. One or two shrubs, but for eight months of the year they're just little mounds of snow. No sound. And then I heard a Raven calling. Even in the most unlikely of places and, however inhospitable it seems, you're never far from a bird. You'll find a bird called a Sandgrouse in the middle of the Sahara Desert, and they have special belly feathers that allow them to soak up water like a sponge, so when they travel back from a water hole back to their nesting site, they can share the water with their family. This is one of the beauties of birds. They're everywhere. And if you can't see them, you'll probably hear them.

When someone asks me what it is I love about birds, my first answer is that they can fly. I still find myself staring at their wings and thinking, *how on earth can you do that?!* Then when I hold one in my hands, like an injured Sedge Warbler, I think, *you're tiny and weigh nothing, but in three months' time, you will have made it past the Sahara Desert into central Africa. I can't walk to the end of the street without huffing and puffing!* You'd think they'd need the size and energy of an elephant to cope with the amount of weight they're going to lose on that sort of journey. The scientific side of how birds are able to cope with these feats of endurance amazes and baffles me. And then when I look at a bird through a pair of binoculars, I think, *Damn, you're beautiful.*

One of the real joys of watching birds (or 'birding', as we call it) is that you can do it anywhere, whether you're in your garden, in the countryside, at the beach or right in the middle of a city centre. If you take the time to stop and listen, you'll find that the world is full of song. Then, if someone with a bit of knowledge about birds helps show you how they birdwatch, you might end up with a completely different relationship with places you know well. That could be a park, a garden, a wood, a churchyard, a beach – even a rooftop or a car park. You'll see the world through different eyes. And it might bring you as much joy as it's brought me.

After I've shown people a few tips and tricks on where to see birds, I often get messages. One such message said, 'I felt like I was a muggle before you showed me how much there is going on beneath the surface!' Suddenly, you're not just seeing Pigeons and Crows, although both of these are incredible for their own reasons. You'll also be seeing beautiful birds like Jays, Nuthatches, Green Woodpeckers and Parakeets. And when you take a minute to properly look at a bird you might already be familiar with, you start to find all sorts of other unexpected gems too. A Magpie just looks black and white, right, with a long tail? But if you really look, you'll see that its feathers shine with greens, blues and purples. And its tail, when it's fanned out, looks like a diamond or a spear. This kind of knowledge can be infectious. Before you know it, you want to see another bird, one that's maybe harder to find or more secretive. So your adventure in birding begins!

When you're looking at buying a new or second-hand car and you've got an idea of what you want, suddenly everything you see on the road is that car! It's a kind of confirmation bias that draws your attention to something without you even knowing it. That's what I want this book to be and its what often happens once people get the bird bug. You might find that you're pointing out birds without even realising it, or passionately explaining some of their unique habits or characteristics to other people. Friends are always telling me how happy they are that they saw a bird they've never seen before. And it's free joy! You don't have to pay for a personal trainer, shell out a small fortune to see something at the cinema or buy that app everyone's talking about. It's all just out there, waiting for you to find it.

And once you're into birds, it can take you in all sorts of different directions, whether you begin to fall in love with other animals or start trying to make your garden or local parks more biodiverse to attract different types of wildlife. It's for this reason that I feel birds are the gateway to the natural world.

But I know that birding isn't for everyone. My brother's wife is terrified of them (!) but my enthusiasm has rubbed off on my nieces and nephews and they've taken me on walks near them and shown me some of the birds on their patch. Birding is sometimes seen to be a solitary activity, but it doesn't need to be. Especially after Covid lockdowns, lots of people have started birding as a family, all enjoying the wonders of being outdoors together. That's one of the reasons the Royal Society for the Protection of Birds (RSPB) 'Big Garden Birdwatch' was such a big success when everyone was at home.

My own mum, bless her, isn't really a bird fan, but she loves how passionate I am about them. One day in my early 20s, when I was still living with my parents in Northampton, I was filming a bird out of a window in our kitchen and my mum asked me what I was up to. So I told her. The next morning, my mum wakes me up, really early in the morning, like 5am, so excited.

'Hamza, Hamza! That chicken you've been looking at is just outside!'

'The...the what, Mum?' I said, through half-opened eyes.

'The chicken, Hamza. The green chicken you were filming yesterday!' she answered.

'The green chicken?' I said, beginning to wonder if I was actually still asleep. 'Mum, I was filming a Green Woodpecker yesterday.'

'Yes, yes, whatever it is. The one that was hoovering up the ants.'

Now, whenever I see a Green Woodpecker, I think of my mum!

I don't know everything about birds, but I love learning things. And the day that I stop learning is the day that I stop living. If you get out there and start looking at nature, the chances are that you'll enjoy it. And if you enjoy it, you'll start to learn things. Then, you'll find yourself looking up information on YouTube, *Springwatch* and Attenborough documentaries. Seeing how passionate the kinds of presenters you'll find on these shows are will probably help inspire you. And you can always look online to find groups of people who are interested in the same things as you are. I guarantee you'll meet people who know things you don't know and want to share them. I have friends who I've got interested in birds and then sometimes they surprise me with something they've found out that I had no idea about. I love it when that happens – the student becomes the teacher! My work is done.

Moving from Sudan

I spent the first eight years of my life in Sudan, in north Africa, which is such a beautiful, amazing place, but quite desolate. Our house was situated on the banks of the River Nile in Khartoum, the capital of Sudan. I grew up surrounded by so many birds, which we knew by their African names. They were so bright and made lots of noise and I had no idea that they were special – they were just our common birds to me. And when we moved to the UK when I was eight – my parents are both doctors and were invited by the Royal College of Medicine to move here – I did miss it there. But then I began to realise that there was so much to offer to a young boy obsessed with Mother Nature. Northumberland was so green, so vibrant, so lush, by comparison to the dry heat and the dust of Sudan and it was a massive shock. It was winter when I arrived in the UK and I was surprised at how cold it was, but I've grown to prefer the cold to the heat, unlike every other member of my family. I actually used to get nosebleeds in Sudan pretty much every day when I overheated, so maybe something's telling me to head north! I still speak Arabic and seem to be good at it because if someone from Sudan rings up for my mum or dad, they're convinced it's my dad talking on the phone, not me. And then when I tell them I'm not Dr Yassin, they say 'But you haven't got an accent – how does that happen?!' That's all thanks to my parents – they spoke Arabic when I was at home and we'd go back to Sudan for summer holidays. It's a bit more difficult when I go back now that I'm older though, because I'm at an age where a lot of people get married, so my grandmother is always on a mission to find me a wife!

My first school was Star of the Sea on Tyneside. I didn't speak any English, but I remember standing up when our teacher came in for my first lesson – that's what we did in Sudan as a mark of respect, although I got some weird looks on that first day for doing it in a primary school in Northumberland! But you learn fast when you have to. You adapt to your surroundings, and that meant without realising it, I developed a Geordie accent for a while.

I remember being asked by a kid at my school what pets I had at home. I said 'We used to have a monkey,' and I'll never forget his little face lighting up with a mixture of disbelief and wonder. I realised that I'd been exposed to a few more creatures than just cats and dogs where I was growing up. But I knew nothing about the wildlife in the UK until I started watching nature shows on TV. I got to see two people that were absolutely amazing – Steve Irwin and David Attenborough. And that was it. From that point on, I wanted to be them, and failing that, the next best thing: the guy holding the camera filming them do what they do. Steve Irwin's enthusiasm was so infectious. He was excited by everything, and I loved that, especially animals that everyone's afraid of. He just had no fear at all, and I think he did a lot to make people understand how crocodiles behave. And then, you've got David Attenborough, with his engaging but laid-back sort of style, presenting to camera while being groomed by a family of gorillas. He was just so fascinating and funny. It always felt like he was talking directly to you.

I owe a lot to both of them. I feel like they sparked the love of nature in me that set me off on the journey to become a wildlife cameraman. One of my favourite memories is a phone call from my friend Jessie, who I'd worked with filming a sequence of White-tailed Eagles hunting Geese. He said: 'I thought you might like to know that David's watched our film of Eagles and said it was a really strong piece.'

I said: 'David? David who? What – wait; you don't mean *Sir* David?!'

That was a massive milestone for me. We're a three-generation team of cameramen: John is the veteran cameraman, Jessie used to be his assistant and I suppose I'm the young buck. In that moment, I wanted to be able to do the same thing for the next generation. I want to inspire kids to say, 'Daddy, can we walk to school instead of drive?' or 'Can we build a bug hotel in the garden?' Because if you connect with kids in this way, I always think to myself, *I might be talking to the future head of the RSPB or the next Attenborough.*

I spent all the time I could out in RSPB reserves when I was young. It was the safest place my mum could take me to. The golden rule in our house growing up was: 'stay out for as long as you like, keep out of trouble, but when the street lights come on, we want you home!'

My parents were really comfortable leaving my brother and me outdoors and letting us have a bit of freedom.

And I think it was that freedom which built up my love for nature and birds, especially. I was fond of the birds I remembered from Sudan. But I really wanted to learn about all the birds we had in the UK. And as soon as I told my mother that, she found out all about the RSPB and learned that there was a reserve near us. The first time I went there, I remember just sitting in a corner of a hide reading a book quietly, then studying the pictures on the walls and the leaflets you'd get there and try and work out which birds I was looking at. Eventually, one of the birders kindly offered me his binoculars because he was looking through his telescope. The next time I went, my mum had got me a cheap pair of binoculars (which I still have!) and she'd come along and read a book in the car while I sat in the hides. You'd see the same guys in the hides and they'd look at me like 'Ah, there's that Hamza guy, we recognise him'. So I'd feel comfortable chatting to them and they were happy with each of the hundred questions I'd throw at them! I loved what they taught me. Eventually, when I got older and a bit more responsible, my mum would just drop me off in the car outside the entrance to the reserve and go off about her daily business. She'd pick me up at the end of the day, ask me what I did and I'd be rattling off a whole list of birds that I saw and facts that I'd learned. She could really see the joy on my face.

Being out at RSPB reserves ticked a lot of boxes for her because it's not exactly the kind of place you can get up to mischief in. I'm out with Mother Nature and a few middle-aged dads with binoculars who took me under their wing and started teaching me the Latin names for things. That was where I learned *Troglodytes troglodytes*, the Latin name for a Wren. I remember finding out that troglodyte was Greek for 'cave-dweller' and came about because Wrens nest in dark crevices. It made sense to me because you never see a Wren's nest out in the open. I get how using Latin names can be off-putting for some people. When people use them, it sort of sounds like they're showing off their knowledge or something. But the helpful thing about Latin is that it's a common language that you can draw on when you go to non-English-speaking countries. It's also useful because it tells you something about the different bird families. For example, if it starts with *Fringillidae*, you know you're talking about a member of the Finch family. If you see *Alba* or *Albus* in a name, you know the bird is going to be at least partly white. Don't worry – I'm not suggesting you take a crash course in Latin, or anything, but being familiar with a few Latin terms gives you that little more information about the bird.

Because my mum and dad were both doctors, they'd be moving across different hospitals around the country on clinical rotations, so we'd have to move house every year or six months. So, while my teachers at school began to suspect I had a problem with reading and writing,

I'd be off to another school before anything could really be done about it. When we first arrived in the UK, we started in Newcastle, then Carlisle, then Whitehaven, then back to Newcastle before we dotted around the Midlands for a bit. It was only when my mum was offered a permanent position in Northampton that we settled there. And it made sense to move there. My parents wanted to be somewhere fairly close to Heathrow, because we did have lots of friends and family visiting from Sudan, but also somewhere that was in the countryside where we kids could all be in the same school. The only trouble was, my dad was on a placement at the Royal Preston Hospital, so he had to stay up north for work and come down to Northampton every weekend. He spent a lot of time yo-yoing around. That's just the way it goes in medical families, though, because it's really hard to both find jobs in the same place at the same time. But, after a few years, a job finally came up in the same Northampton hospital, so were all together again under the same roof all the time.

At the first school I went to in Northampton, you had to take an entrance exam, which involved mostly English with a bit of maths and science. I aced the maths and science, but massively stuffed up the English. I got in, but the teachers said that I'd have to work hard on my English. So I wasn't able to study French or History – I spent the time taking extra English lessons. I basically ended up in a special needs class, until my mum took me out, and got me a place at another school – Wellingborough. In lessons, I'd be there at the front of the class with my hand up and the answer ready, but in exams I failed everything. I loved the school and got on so well with my teachers, but I found the reading and writing so difficult. After I'd take an exam, my teacher would say, 'Were you ill for the exam or something? I know you know this stuff!' And I'd say, 'No – I thought I did pretty well!' It was then that my teacher, Mrs Strange, diagnosed me with dyslexia.

I remember crying when she told me I was dyslexic. I'd never heard of it before and at first, it sounded like a really serious physical condition. But she told me kindly that it means it's hard for me to read and write. Everything began to make sense. I wasn't dumb, like I sometimes feared – I just think and do things slightly differently. Mrs Strange informed me the school would be able to help support me with a computer, a reader and a scribe – which was amazing. Thinking about it now, I genuinely believe that we dyslexics have a gift that other people don't see. I realise that I see and feel the world in a different way to other people and I've got to the point where I'm glad I'm dyslexic. I find it difficult to read, but I've managed to work out ways around that. I listen to podcasts, the audio content in apps about nature, watch documentaries, look through photographs. It feels like I've learned to read again, but in a different way.

I look up to amazing people like Whoopi Goldberg, Robin Williams and Octavia Spencer who have used their dyslexia to their advantage. Whoopi wasn't diagnosed until adulthood, but she realised that she learned best by having someone read things out loud to her, and she wouldn't have a problem remembering them. So after she became an actress, that's how she learned her lines. Now she's one of only 18 EGOT winners – the acronym for people who have won an Emmy, Grammy, Oscar and Tony Award. She's a legend. She found a way of adjusting and working around something she was struggling with. That's how I feel about dyslexia. We're faced with having to get from A to B and we find a way around. We learn to adapt, and that often involves thinking creatively. And on that journey, maybe you find new things about yourself or develop new skills.

Following My Dream

Although I had this desire to become David Attenborough or Steve Irwin, I did briefly want to become the character Leroy Johnson from the film (and spin-off TV show) *Fame* (for those of you too young for this reference, it's an American teen musical set in a New York performing arts high school). I remember watching in awe the famous scene where he did the jumping splits and I thought, *right, that's it – that's what I'm going to do*. So I trained hard at gymnastics and learned how to do it. I was so happy! But I think my life was always going to involve nature. I knew how much I loved spending time outdoors looking at birds, first in Sudan, then the UK. And I've carried a camera around with me pretty much every day since I got my first one, aged 12. It was a birthday present from my mum and it was a Fuji with a 35mm film. I've still got it at my parents' place. I remember I'd had it for about two hours, though, and it stopped working. So I took it in to show my mum:

'Mum, my camera's stopped working!'

'What do you mean, Hamza?'

'The click button isn't clicking anymore, and the flash isn't going off.'

'Well, you've filled it up – you've taken all the 36 pictures on the film. Now we need to take it to a place to develop it, so we can see the pictures. But each time we do this, it costs us money, and it takes a wee while to get the pictures back.'

'Ah.'

It turned out that every click worked out as 50p, which was my week's pocket money! And at that point in my life, 50p meant 50 penny sweets from the newsagent. So I had an agonising decision to make: *do I want to take a picture or do I want a bag of sweets?!*

So from snapping everything I saw in the space of two hours, I'd learn to only take a picture when something really cool came up, whether that was family, friends, pets or the swans by the park. The next film we developed (Mum paid for that one) was a month and a half later and the images were curated a bit better! I remember limiting myself to a certain number of pictures for each bird, though. And then digital came along. When I first heard about it, it didn't sound that impressive, until someone at school said, 'You can take a thousand pictures on it.'

That was it. 'Mum,' I said, 'I need a new camera.'

I was 14 when she bought me my first digital camera, another Fuji. I could fill cards to my heart's content, run through them on my computer, keep the ones I wanted, and delete the rest. I was in paradise. I've had a few cameras, but now, whenever I'm going to Africa on a shoot, I'll take a couple of my old digital cameras and give them to the guides to say thank you for their help. Because more often than not, guides absolutely love the natural world, but they might not have the means to capture what they love. When I ask them if they'd like the camera, I ask them to stay in touch and send me pictures, and a lot of them still do. Sometimes I get messages telling me that they've upgraded their camera but they've passed it on to their son or daughter and they've fallen in love with photography. It makes me so happy, that kind of thing.

I knew what I wanted to do with my life, but there was something else weighing on my shoulders. I come from a long line of doctors and dentists (both my parents are

Obstetrics/Gynaecology doctors, and at that point my sister was on her way to become a GP and my brother on the path to become a dentist) and I felt like this is what my parents wanted me to do. They never said anything like 'you should be a dentist', but it seemed like I was being subliminally guided towards it! So I found myself following my siblings and choosing biology, chemistry, physics and maths for my A levels before applying for Dentistry courses at university. I knew that my struggles with reading and writing were always going to be an issue because there were all sorts of essays that I'd need to write for a medical course, but I figured I'd find a way to adapt and overcome these challenges. I wanted my parents to be proud of me, so I sent off the forms and, to my surprise, I got into a couple of unis.

But then, four months before I was due to start on the Dentistry course, I just couldn't face it. So I plucked up the courage and had the conversation with my parents. Thankfully, they were really understanding, proud of me for finding the courage to come and talk to them honestly about it. They told me that they wanted me to choose what I wanted to do, not what they thought might be good for me, and that they'd support whatever decision I wanted to take. So I said: 'Mum and Dad – I want to work with animals as a wildlife cameraman and I know that you need to have a degree in Zoology to be taken seriously.' They told me they'd support me

100 per cent. And that had such a powerful impact. Not only did I feel like a great weight had been lifted off my shoulders, I also felt properly excited. I set out straight away, trying to find a degree that combined my two passions – wildlife and photography. The one I liked the sound of most was Zoology with Conservation and Animal Behaviour that Bangor University was offering. Plus, Bangor is incredibly well situated, on the north Wales coast, for marine wildlife and birds. Just across the water, on Anglesey, you've got the well-known birding hotspots of South Stack, Puffin Island and the beaches of Rhosneigr, and just ten miles south, you've got Snowdon, the highest mountain in England and Wales, and the unique wildlife around it. Bangor is surrounded by all the wildlife you could hope to study or learn about, so you find yourself learning about animals and then jumping on a coach for a field trip the next week and actually seeing them within an hour or two. And, on top of all that, people kept telling me that if you're dyslexic and you want to go to uni, Bangor is a great option because their Dyslexia Team was the best in the UK. They'd even won an award for it that year. I visited two other universities, but when I came to Bangor for the Open Day, I knew immediately that this was the place for me. And it's proved to be one of the best decisions I've ever made. It felt like a course that has made me who I am.

I was the first one in the lecture theatre, sat there right at the front with my Dictaphone, because I knew I wouldn't be able to keep up with the writing. The amazing guys in the Dyslexia Team gave me what I called the 'Madonna Mic', a device that allows you to sing along or speak into it, while it writes your dissertation down for you. I also got the use of a laptop with specialised software and the help of both a reader and a scribe, like at Wellingborough, and they were amazing. It felt like we'd formed a really collaborative relationship, and it really helped me work closely with other people. When it came to writing essays, I dictated what I wanted to say and then I worked with the Dyslexia Team to tidy up parts that didn't make sense, add the correct grammar, that sort of thing. They were incredible, and it's one reason I go back each year to give talks to the students at Bangor Uni about how I followed my dream and became a cameraman.

I was lucky because I knew exactly what I wanted to do after graduation, so I went about getting as much camera experience as I could. I love sports. I'd played a lot of rugby at school and I made the Bangor Uni Rugby team, but an idea struck me. What if I photographed as many of the other sports teams playing their matches at uni as I could? It sharpened up my hand-eye coordination and helped me anticipate things that are about to happen. I've since learned that there's no real set way to become a cameraman or camerawoman – if you ask anyone in the business, you find out that everyone's arrived at it from all sorts of directions. A lot of it is about who you know rather than what you know, because personal recommendations go a long way, but once you get that opportunity to deliver, you've just got to take it.

I fell in love with the people and the place straight away up in Bangor. One person I met there, who's had a big impact on my life, is my friend Chris Bridge. I first met him, late at night, clanking around as he was carrying a big tripod through Bangor Uni. I asked him what he'd been out shooting.

'I'm a birder,' he said. 'I've been out bird ringing.'

In case you don't know (I didn't at the time) bird ringing involves safely and gently catching birds and fitting tiny rings with identification tags to their feet or wings so we can study population and survival rates, feeding patterns, lifespans, migration patterns and incidences of disease like avian flu, among other things. Bird ringing is something you need a permit for as well as a licence to catch wild birds, as well as permission from the landowner, if necessary.

Chris and I hit it off straight away. I told him next time he went out bird ringing, he was taking me with him. Chris knew as much as some of the older birders I'd hung out with in RSPB reserves, but he was a fellow young'un, so I naturally gravitated towards him. His mum and dad used to carry him on their backs when they were going on birding trips, so his whole life has revolved around birds. He taught me a lot and got me into twitching (travelling sometimes serious distances to see a particular bird). And part of the reason I think he did that was because he couldn't drive! A year after we met, we moved into a shared house together outside uni, and he used to tap on my wall at like 3am and then whisper, 'Hamza! Are you awake?' And before I'd reply, he'd excitedly follow it up with something like, 'There's a bird in Anglesey!' after getting an alert in one of his groups. And I'd say, sleepily, through the wall, 'Is it a pretty bird, Chris?' because I'm a photographer and I'd always be thinking about the pictures, even when I'm half asleep. The next question I'd ask though, before grabbing the car keys was, 'Is it close? Or are we talking a telescope on top of a telescope to see it?'

I ended up going on a few twitches, but I was much more interested in bird ringing. Chris introduced me to a couple of specialised techniques: cannon netting (which involves firing nets high over birds so the net is lifted safely over a flock before everyone sprints to the net to remove the birds as quickly as you can, cover them in a light material to calm them, then examine them) and mist netting (a similar technique, but the net is held between two poles and the birds fly into it). Bird ringing is another level of birding because you're able to hold and examine birds that you'd only ever otherwise see at the end of a telescope. And that massively appealed to me because instead of seeing a fleeting glimpse of a bird through binoculars or a scope, you're able to really study it in your hand. How its flight feathers are arranged. How much they weigh (it always surprises people how little they weigh, even birds like Tawny Owls). And when you've got a bird like a Firecrest in your hand, you can't even feel the weight. It's less than a 20p coin and yet it's capable of flying thousands of miles. It's only when I held a creature like this safely in my hand that I really appreciated how phenomenal that ability is.

My first bird-ringing trip involved ringing Shelducks, which are large, beautiful ducks. Before I knew it, someone had passed me a Shelduck and then another, so I'm suddenly holding a duck under each arm.

'What do I do with them?!' I asked.

'Hold the head up and the feet out!' someone shouted.

'OK,' I said, still not really sure.

It's a bit like when someone passes you a baby and says: 'Hold the head,' and you don't know what they're talking about until you're actually holding one. Then you get it. That day, I learned how to put a ring on a duck, how to read the numbers on the rings and how to take the various measurements they needed. I'd never been that close to a bird, and it was such a thrill. After I'd ringed one of the Shelducks, I was told to sign a form and then give the bird a name.

'It's your first bird, Hamza – they've always got to have a name!'

We were in North Wales, so I came up with the name of a valley, but someone told me it had to be something a bit shorter and more memorable.

And then an older volunteer said, in a deadpan voice, 'Call it Krusty.'

'Krusty the Shelduck it is,' I said, and wrote it down. And then, when I looked back up, everyone was pissing themselves with laughter before patting me on the back. It was a lovely, funny community and a world I was just beginning to get a taste for. It's something I'd recommend to anyone who's getting into birds because there really is nothing like seeing a bird that close. There's no textbook that can teach you the things you'll discover and you come out with a whole new appreciation for how incredible these little creatures truly are. And there are bird-ringing groups all over the UK.

So, after having the kinds of incredible experiences I had at uni on my course and with friends like Chris, it was hard to head home to Northampton each summer, because you go straight back to being a kid again when you're at home. It's tricky because you love your mum and dad, but you love your new independence and you want more of it! After I'd graduated from Bangor, my parents wanted to know what I was going to do next. In fairness, so did I! I remember my dad asking me why I didn't just get a job in Next or something like that in the short term, but I didn't want to do that. I wanted to be a wildlife cameraman, so it seemed like the best thing to do was to go back into education to take a Masters, and I found a course that I liked the sound of, in Biological Photography and Imaging at the University of Nottingham. I loved that and when I got back the next summer, I knew I had to work out how I was going to make this dream happen. That started by saying yes to a friend's kind offer.

A Whole New World

I'd met this friend on my undergraduate course. She had been going to a place in Scotland with her parents for years, and kept inviting me, but I'd always say 'maybe in a few months' or 'maybe next year'. Then, when I went to stay with her at her family home in Yorkshire and saw this stunning photograph of a stag in their lounge, I asked where they took it. 'Ardnamurchan. The place I've been telling you about! Dad took the picture just outside the car on his phone,' she answered.

'No, no, no – this has to be with a zoom lens,' I said.

'Nope – the stag was just over there,' she said, pointing about 3 metres away.

'When are you going there next?!' I asked.

'Three weeks.'

'I'm coming with you.'

It did take a while to get to Ardnamurchan, but that's part of the beauty of it. It's a peninsula, unlike any other, and is home to the most westerly point on the mainland. On my first day there, I just walked around with my mouth open. I was in awe of everything around me. And then I saw a Golden Eagle. There was something so special about the place. I knew it was where I was going to learn to become a cameraman. It also kind of made sense, because all the filming that I'd been doing so far was in North Wales or Scotland. And I thought, *why am I living in Northampton? If I moved to Scotland, I'd be a few hours away from jobs, max.*

With that in mind, I returned home, and two weeks later, I moved up there for good.

I spent the first week trying to convince my parents that I wanted to live in Scotland. They were asking me all the sensible questions parents ask, like, *how are you going to fund yourself? What are you going to do for a job? Where are you going to live?* And I told them I'd found a spot, which wasn't untrue. It was just that the spot I found was a car park and I'd be sleeping in my car! The second week, I spent packing my car with all the essentials I was going to need. My dad was certain this was just a phase I was going through and that after I'd used up the washing powder I'd taken with me, I'd be straight back home. Well, it's been 12 years now and that phase is still going, I guess!

I didn't have a job or a place to live when I drove up there. But I knew where I wanted to be and felt like I was living the dream. I ended up parking my car (it was a big seven-seater) in the ferry terminal car park right next to the big yellow 'No Overnight Parking or Camping' sign so no one could see it! I spent the first six months there, usually moving the car every morning before 8 o'clock, when people would start using the car park. But I imagine people were asking themselves, 'Who the hell is sleeping next to the pier?!'

But I had everything I needed there. The toilet block was next door and there were showers just down the road. I put my shoes under the car each night before I turned in for the night in case it rained. And to be fair, they were pretty stinky – way too stinky to join me in my luxury accommodation. There was a nice pub a few minutes away which I'd drive to to use the Wi-Fi and for meals (I had chicken nuggets and chips so much, I think the landlord just came over and asked if I wanted 'the usual' after a couple of days!). I had this rough plan to stay at the hotel for a couple of nights and then find my own place, but that didn't end up happening. I was quite happy in my car! The pub – the Kilchoan Hotel – is the only watering hole for 22 miles, so if anyone in the area says 'We're going out', you know exactly where they're headed! It's a time-warp of a pub but I love it, right down to its heavily worn 70s carpets, plates hanging on the wall, tartan everywhere. That was my life for nine months until I started working for the Kilchoan estate as a ghillie – a right-hand man to someone stalking game, basically. You do the dirty jobs, like skinning, that the stalker doesn't want to do.

For me, it was money I needed. I didn't really want to see animals shot, but I did make an exception for Red Deer on the west coast because the population was out of control, to the extent that it's still affecting the ecosystem today. Trees aren't growing, and new saplings get bitten back as soon as they're planted. As a ghillie, you've got to learn how to approach animals quietly and that's something I've taken with me into my camera work. I also cut grass and chopped logs for people, which was easy because many of the cottages are holiday homes, so I'd just needed to make sure everything was ready for the new guests. I started doing house cleaning as well for new guests coming in. I started with one house and was soon doing three, which was great because it paid £50 a house. I worked out that I needed £100 a month to survive, which was enough for my petrol (because I didn't move much around the village) and for food. I was earning enough to make a mini-living out of it, and even started being able to save up for equipment I needed, like a new lens.

I moved into a caravan – one that you tow on the back of the car – which the stalker I worked with on the estate offered me. It had been left inside a shed for years and was full of mouse droppings, but he told me that if I wanted to clean it out, I could stay in it for a few nights. I was still in there two years later! There was no running water or heating, but I had two big hoodies and two duvets, and that kept me warm enough. I remember in the winter having the same conversation with myself each night: *Do you want to pee now or wait until the middle of the night?* Either way, it was pretty chilly, but at least if you went out straight away you get that over and done with. And that was life for me. Surviving.

During the day, I'd be walking the hills, filming birds, looking for nests, searching for otter holts (dens) – trying to cut my teeth as a wildlife cameraman. My binoculars are always attached to me by a mini-harness, but I wasn't going to lug all my camera equipment everywhere looking for wildlife and then take pictures. If you do it that way, you'll be absolutely knackered within two days and having a big argument with your camera. What you do is do your research beforehand. You see a Barn Owl coming out of an outbuilding and you stop to investigate, or 'inspectorgate' as I call it, and you find loads of owl pellets. So I'd put up barn owl boxes, fill the boxes with the owl pellets, because that's what they use for their nesting material, and then next year, they'll hopefully use it for their nests.

After that, I'd sit down and make a list of all the animals I could think of attracting. Sadly, quite a few deer get hit by cars up in the Scotland, and especially around Rannoch Moor, a beautiful area of moorland near Glen Coe. But it presented me with an opportunity – I wondered if I could use the meat to feed eagles. So I started doing night-time drive-bys to pick up and recycle roadkill. I mean, I must have looked like a murderer, turning up in famous beauty spots in the dead of night and heaving bodies from A to B. But it proved to be a gamble worth taking because I soon found myself just a few metres away from Golden Eagles. And they happily took the meat, so I got to have these extraordinary experiences sitting just feet away from one of the most incredible birds of prey in the world. I'd stick the camera on, but I wouldn't even need to look through it – I could see them with my own eyes in incredible detail. And I was just thinking, *this is phenomenal. How on earth is this even possible?*

A year after putting together the owl boxes, a couple of Barn Owls moved in, and it was such an incredible feeling, especially when the eggs hatched. It only took a year to get those shots, which in wildlife photography terms, is nothing!

Over time, I've become a sort of Dr Doolittle in Ardnamurchan, helping treat injured animals and pets.

Anything that moves will basically end up at my place, which has become a sort of unofficial animal rehabilitation centre. I do my best, but my speciality is birds. My training as a bird ringer means I know how to handle birds so as not to hurt them. Beyond that, though, I get called in for any heavy lifting people need in the community, which has earned me the nickname 'the Walking Forklift'. But the way people ask for help up here is really sweet. They tend to invite me over for dinner and then mention that they might need a bit of help moving the Aga. There's a real sense of family, camaraderie and community, and I've found a place among them. There's a famous saying in Africa: It takes a village to raise a child. It's taken a village to help me become the wildlife cameraman that I am now. Everyone helps each other out.

I can see White-tailed Eagles, Golden Eagles, Whinchats, Ringed Plovers, Redshanks and Curlews just outside my window. Granted, it is a big window looking out to sea, but there are so many different habitats within that view and it fills me with joy. I still think, *What the hell!* every time. It blows my mind. I love seeing how they live throughout the seasons, in different weathers. I usually see a pair of Mallards that nest in the reeds in front of the house, and I see they have ten chicks. The next day, though, they might have only eight, and I can't help but feel sad. Then a week later, I see that they still have eight, and I'm instinctively filled with joy. I know that they're not all going to last, though, and that two or three will probably survive, but that's exactly why the Mallards will have ten to twelve chicks each time. Several of them will be taken by birds of prey as well as Herons, otters and mink. It's all part of a chain and keeps those others feeding their families and surviving. The time the Mallard chicks have reached juvenile stage, there will be two or three to start up the next generation. Beyond the Mallards in the reeds, I can see the local otter family on the edge of the bay shaking the water off their fur to keep themselves warm. And then, in the distance, I can sometimes see dolphins and minke whales. It's funny, because at first glance, this area can look pretty barren, but if you know where to look and the places to go, you'll start falling in love with it. I can see something from my living room and be filming it within 90 seconds. This is where I want to be, surrounded by the wildlife I love. Nowhere else can you see a minke whale, a dolphin, an otter, an adder and an Eagle on the same day.

A Lucky Break

Studying in North Wales for my undergraduate degree, I managed to get the number of an amazing wildlife cameraman called Jesse Wilkinson from a friend of a friend. I did my research, sent him a message telling him I wanted to be a wildlife cameraman and asked him if he'd help and advise me. As a bit of a sweetener,

I mentioned that I was a big dude, an ex-rugby player and that I could carry his gear for him. He wrote back saying thank you, but he usually works alone because it is kind of a solitary job and suggested contacting the BBC. I thanked him, but then a couple of weeks later, he phoned me up. It caught me a bit off guard to be honest because he said 'Hi Hamza, it's Jesse', and it took me a good few seconds to realise it was Jesse Wilkinson. He told me he'd injured his back, and would be grateful if he could take me up on my offer! I ended up becoming his assistant for a few years, and it was such an incredible experience. He found out about my love for birds and the fact I could identify them very quickly and one day he asked if I knew a nearby plucking post – which is like a tree stump or something similar – where a bird of prey returns after catching something, to remove the feathers before eating it. He wanted to use it for an upcoming sequence.

Well, it just so happened that I did know one nearby that I'd seen a Sparrowhawk using, but I said, 'Nope Jesse – it's my secret place!'

'Attenborough's going to be narrating over the top of the footage,' he replied.

'Well, why didn't you say?!'

It turned out it was going to be a TV show called *The Hunt*, a BBC nature documentary that came out in 2015 about the relationship between predators and their prey.

I worked as a camera assistant. Everything took off from there really, helping each other out on jobs, all thanks to a dodgy back and me putting myself out there and taking a chance.

It's never felt like a job to me. It feels more like I'm being paid to do a hobby I love. 'Find a job you enjoy doing, and you will never have to work a day in your life' is an old saying I live by.

My advice to young people who want to become wildlife cameramen and women is to contact everyone you can find who does it for a job and ask if you can help and learn from them. The worst they can say is no. But someone will be grateful for the offer of help at some point and then you'll have the opportunity. And once you're there, you're getting the most valuable training there is – being an apprentice to someone skilled in a profession you already love. The other advice, which I'd borrowed from someone I admire greatly, formed the speech I gave to the graduating students at Bangor Uni, my alma mater, in July 2022. I'm still flabbergasted that I got a call to say that they wanted to award me an honorary Master of Science degree. And that news was made even more special because I knew that my hero, David Attenborough, had received one of the uni's first honorary degrees in 2009. The three pieces of advice (given by American actor, singer, dancer and choreographer André De Shields during his acceptance speech after receiving the Key to the City of Baltimore in 2019, just two months after winning his first Tony Award at the age of 73) were:

1. Surround yourself with people whose eyes light up when they see you coming.
2. Slowly is the fastest way to get to where you want to be.
3. The top of one mountain is the bottom of the next, so keep climbing!

When I'm working, I'm giving it 100 per cent, I always do, whether I'm staying alert for hours at a time in a hide or giving a talk to a group of kids. But the truth is, when I'm not working, I'm a bit lazy! I love my bed and I love sleeping. So I'll wake up late, see what's happening outside and maybe do a bit of filming. It's the complete opposite when I'm commissioned to work as a cameraman on a project. If it's summer, I'm usually up at 2.30am, out of the house by 3am and I'm probably getting back home at 10pm.

And you might be dealing with long hikes carrying heavy equipment, long waits in a hide and even in summer, when you're not moving, it will get cold. You train yourself to adapt to these new surroundings though, teaching yourself to become more and more patient and learning to keep your concentration level up. The way I tend to think about it is if I switch off and I miss the crucial few minutes of footage, not only will I have wasted however much time I will have been in a hide, I'm also not going to get paid!

Most people think that hides are really big and posh-looking – like the ones you get at nature reserves – where you can stretch and move around, but the ones we actually use on shoots are tiny, usually a 1m x 1m cube where you're sitting sideways on a little tripod stool. I make my own hides out of wooden pallets, one of which is at an angle with a hole cut out for the front. You wrap a waterproof membrane around and then cover with vegetation. The one I made to shoot the White-tailed Eagles near me my friend and I built into a section of collapsed dry stone wall; we camouflaged the hide by rebuilding the wall around it. The animals will know there's a drystone wall there already, so they might register that something's changed slightly, but not enough to spook them. The hide has to be small so that the animal barely notices it. Plus, if it's bigger, you have to work even harder to camouflage it.

Living in a hide does take a bit of getting used to and requires more concentration than you might think. The first time I was inside a hide by myself I went along with my headphones but I realised I was constantly getting distracted. It's the same thing if you try and read a book – you lose focus on the animals. You also don't want to be too comfortable because you might nod off.

And you don't want to miss any giveaway behaviour from a chick that they're about to do something or from an adult Golden Eagle who's suddenly focusing on something in the distance intently. So, you have to have all your senses switched on because at some point, something's going to happen and you don't know when, but you do know you have to be ready to catch it when it does. I've learned that the hard way, watching a Red-Throated Diver incubating her eggs and thinking it'd be a good time to take a break, because I was expecting her to just sit on the egg for the next six hours, as she had been for the past few days. But then, she got up, and the chick started to crack the egg and I wasn't in position to film it. So you learn to sharpen your focus through your mistakes.

It also takes more stamina, preparation and creativity than I imagined. You've got to think about your wellbeing – the last thing you want to be doing is injuring yourself, because you'll be out of the game for a while and you can't afford that, as a freelancer. On the first couple of hide shoots, I was crawling out of the hide with massively swollen legs, so I've learned to wear those pressure socks you wear on aeroplanes or after surgery to stop deep vein thrombosis (DVT). You also have to learn to cope with the boredom and figure out workarounds for problems like hay fever, which I do suffer from. The answer – plugging my nostrils with tissue!

You also want to double-check you've got all of your equipment with you before you leave the car. I've hiked for miles with all my stuff before I've realised I've left the memory cards I need to record the footage onto. Or the tripod I need to mount the camera! I've now got emergency cards that do not leave my bag and if they do, the first thing I do when I get back home is replace them! You develop a routine. I call it the 'idiot check' to make sure I've got everything I need. It's got longer as I've got more experienced, mainly because it includes things learned from previous mistakes I've made. Like remembering to turn the auto-flash feature off on my iPhone. I left that on when I was shooting a pair of Golden Eagles (not my local ones) and wanted to take a cheeky phone snap. I didn't make a sound, but the flash was enough to spook the Eagle, who flew off straight away.

These sorts of things are small sacrifices to get to do what you love: getting to travel the world, seeing the most incredible animals and environments. At the beginning of my career as a wildlife cameraman, I never really thought I'd do any presenting work. But then one of my friends kept telling me that he reckoned I'd be great on camera. I just shrugged it off at first. I thought, *I don't have the right body type or charisma that people are after.* But my friend got in touch with her friend, who was making a programme about up-and-coming wildlife camera operators and she asked me to come down and sent me the address. Little did I know until I arrived that it was *The One Show* on the BBC! After the show, I bumped into an agent (Jan) who was actually waiting for a client of hers there. A few people had already approached me asking if I was represented by anyone, but Jan and I got on so well straight away. She took me out to dinner to discuss it more and I'm glad she did, because she's become a part of my extended family now!

Jan thought I definitely had a personality for TV and started to look for work for me. And soon afterwards, in late 2019, came some unbelievable news. CBeebies wanted to make a show called *Let's Go for a Walk* and had me in mind to present it! And then, in 2020, Channel 4 approached us to make the one-off documentary *Scotland: My Life in the Wild* about my home and the wildlife around me in Ardnamurchan. The following year I was offered guest presenter roles on *Countryfile* and *Animal Park*. I still can't believe any of it, really. It had been an incredible couple of years, it really had.

And then, in the middle of 2022, out of the blue, I got a strange message from my agent Jan.

'Do you like to dance?' it read.

I wondered what she was on about, but I replied: 'Yeah!'

Then she dropped the bombshell on me.

'One of the execs at *Strictly Come Dancing* has been in touch. Have you got a video of you dancing?'

Woah.

I searched everything that I, my friends and family had, but the best I could find was a video from about 2015 someone had taken on their phone at a house party, which we sent over.

Then I was invited to come down and meet the guys at *Strictly* in London. When I did meet them, they said 'Thank God you came down because we wouldn't have picked you based on the video you sent over!' The meeting went really well, but then I didn't hear anything for ages. In the meantime, I'd flown to the Canadian Arctic on a wildlife shoot for a few months. But that was coming to an end, and I was wondering what was next on the horizon, so I messaged Jan from the satellite phone to ask what was happening with *Strictly*. Because if it wasn't going ahead, I needed to know so I could pick up some more camera work! She said 'Give me a week – I'll message you'.

A week later, I got this message:

'You've got *Strictly*. Don't tell a soul!'

Bring it on! The first person I told was a sleeping polar bear under the stars in the middle of nowhere. I couldn't tell any of the humans around, the camera guys or the guides until the news was aired, so I kept completely silent about it. Wow, that was hard! Also, we were struggling to get a hunting sequence shot of a polar bear catching a beluga whale. So it wouldn't have been the best time to drop into conversation that I was heading off to *Strictly*. Three weeks later, we finally got the sequence, and we were all happy with it. So that was the moment I chose to tell everyone. If we hadn't have got the sequence, I would have told everyone after we landed back in the UK, but it felt like a good time to break the news. Suddenly, everyone on the shoot was asking me: 'Hang on a minute – how famous are you, Hamza?! How many followers have you got?' I was like: 'I'm just a dude that does a bit of wildlife camerawork for a living and does a few bits on kids' TV. And a bit of guest stuff on *Countryfile*. It's a surprise to me too!'

Strictly was a whirlwind, and to be honest, I still feel like I'm flying with the birds. I think I experienced every single possible emotion. It was quite a feat of endurance, though. On Mondays, I would start training with my dance partner Jowita for a few hours before heading down to Longleat to film *Animal Park*. Then Tuesday evening, Jowita came down to Longleat so we could carry on training. I'd wake up on Wednesday morning and it was back to filming at Longleat, then training with Jowita in the evening before we drove back to London together. Then we had the whole of Thursday to train.

Being on *Strictly* was the first time I'd ever been to London, apart from picking up grandmothers and aunties from Heathrow Airport. I don't do cities, really! Sometimes the heavens would open and the streets would get an absolute drenching. I think that was the only time I'd seen the streets so peaceful. I love the wind and the rain, and I think I'm built for the wild, really. But even in the middle of a concrete jungle, hanging out with a friend for a coffee, I'd be seeing Parakeets whizz by, Sparrowhawks on the hunt and Peregrine Falcons chasing down Pigeons.

HOW TO USE THIS BOOK

In this book, I've talked about 50 birds, some of which are common and you can see anywhere, and more obscure birds that you can see if you know where to look. Some of these birds only travel to the UK in summer or winter, but that just means you've got a great opportunity to see these amazing visitors, who have probably travelled thousands of miles to get here. I love winter time and part of that is because it's one of the best times to birdwatch. Firstly, you don't have to get up at 2:30 in the morning to get yourself into position, if you're heading to a hide! Also, the lack of leaves can make spotting birds, like Redwings, that bit easier. And it's the time of year when some birds, like ducks or Waxwings come over in large numbers, so it's the best time to see them.

I've split them up into habitat types so if you find yourself by the coast or heathland across the UK or

Europe, you can keep an eye out for birds you might not have heard of, like a Stonechat, or if you're going on a walking trip in the Highlands (good choice, by the way) or mountainous terrain in Europe, get yourself a pair of binoculars (see page 50) and keep your eyes peeled for a Golden Eagle. I want you to take this book with you when you're out and about or back home after a day exploring or at the beach, so you can try and identify the bird you caught a glimpse of today that isn't a House Sparrow, Starling or Robin.

I've added a fact box for each bird including:

- Its scientific name;
- Its conservation status;
- Look (and/or Listen) Out For, which gives you pointers about how to identify them;
- How easy it is to see them, using the scale Easy, Fairly Easy, Tricky and Challenging, based on how common they are, how widespread their numbers are and how visible they like to make themselves;
- A summary of the bird in three words, which was a lot of fun putting together (although sometimes it crept up to four or five words especially for some of my favourite birds; and we counted hyphenated words as one word to make it a bit easier!). I'm not sure anyone else has tried that before in a book about birds!

I've included the conservation status of the birds in the book both in the UK and Europe. For the UK, it's based on a review called *Birds of Conservation Concern*, which is compiled by the UK's leading bird conservation/monitoring organizations. They use a traffic-light system of Red, Amber and Green and the last review was published in 2021. Birds on the Red List are either very rare in the UK or have suffered from severe declines in population sizes. Amber is used to point out birds whose status is of moderate concern, but this isn't always bad news, as some of the species have moved up from the Red List to the Amber List if they show increases in population numbers. Green means that the species isn't showing any signs of moderate or severe declines in numbers. The list as a whole makes for worrying reading, sadly, because more birds are on the Red List than ever before.

The list in Europe is compiled by the organization BirdLife International and follows the IUCN (International Union for Conservation of Nature) guidelines, which places animals in one of eight categories: Least Concern, Near Threatened, Vulnerable, Endangered, Critically Endangered, Regionally Extinct, Extinct in the Wild, and Extinct. The last review was carried out in 2021.

What I'll help you with is, by a process of elimination, how to identify a bird you don't recognise, whatever the habitat type you're in. That's how I do it! And to do that,

I run through a mental checklist. Because to identify a bird, you need to answer at least one of these questions: what does it look like? How big is it? What habitat is it in? What's it doing in that environment? What does it sound like? Time of year is important, too. And even if you can only answer a couple of these questions, you still will have narrowed it down to maybe two or three birds. It's a really satisfying process, like you're a kind of birding Sherlock Holmes, going through the clues until you can identify the culprit!

One other thing: it's become common to put species names in lower-case letters, but it's something I've never understood. It feels like we're somehow devaluing the natural world, especially when brand names and things like cars are capitalised. So we've put the species names in this book in capitals. They're the stars of the show after all. Plus, it means you avoid the kind of confusion you get when we talk about species names that include the word 'Common', 'Little' or 'Great'. 'Little owls can often be seen in the daylight' can be read as both a description of all small owls and a description of one of the specific characteristics of the species the Little Owl. Writing birds' species names with capitals gives them the respect they deserve and it's more sensible!

All the birds I've included are birds I love. Some of them remind me of people, of happy places, or of incredible experiences. Some are surprisingly common, but they've all got a story behind them, whether that's the amazing internal crash helmet of the Great Spotted Woodpecker or the humble and overlooked Blackbird, who's learned to sing at a higher frequency in towns and cities to get his beautiful song across over the noise of the traffic.

Birding isn't just sitting in a hide with a pair of binoculars, waiting for something to happen. It's out there, right in front of you. And a lot of the time you hear them before you see them. Or you see signs that one is approaching, like Pigeons all suddenly taking off all at the same time from a rooftop. In Africa, when the baboons go absolutely nuts, they start making alarm calls and climbing trees very quickly, so you know a leopard is nearby. And after all that commotion, the leopard realises he's been rumbled, so you'll see the tail flick up and he comes out into the open. In Scotland, the Ravens have a specific call that lets each other know that an aerial predator is coming. And the only aerial predators in Scotland that will go after a Raven is a White-tailed Eagle or a Golden Eagle. It's all about recognising a pattern of behaviour that changes the behaviour of another animal. And when you start to become familiar with those patterns, you might be able to predict what kind of bird might be likely to appear.

I've turned it into a bit of a joke now, so that when I'm with friends and I hear the alarm call of a Raven,

I'll look at my watch and say, 'Right, any time now we should see an eagle coming over.' And then an eagle flies overhead and everyone's open-mouthed saying: 'Hamza, how the hell did you know that?' And I'll shrug and say 'Oh yeah, well it's 4:15pm – that is when they turn up each day. They're very regular', before my serious face breaks and I tell them the truth! The thing is, if you get to know a particular environment, you'll find that you can deduce really quickly what's going on when a bird's behaviour changes suddenly. I know that if a group of Pigeons are all suddenly taking off at once from a rooftop in the centre of London, it's probably because they've been startled by a predator. So I start thinking of the birds of prey that could take down a Pigeon: a big Sparrowhawk, a Peregrine Falcon, a Harris Hawk or a Goshawk. Goshawks are woodland birds, so it's not going to be that. You'll only find a Harris Hawk in a city if they've been introduced to control Pigeons and Herring Gulls, so it's probably not that either. Your most likely candidate is a Peregrine Falcon because it's adapted very well to cities and treat Pigeons like fast-food snacks. But they almost always catch birds in flight and come down very quickly from a great height, so it's probably not a Peregrine. So, by a process of elimination, I'm saying it's a Sparrowhawk. I do these kinds of deductions quickly in my head without even really thinking about it. It's a bit like a flowchart where you've got several contenders for what the bird can be, but you rule out each one in turn based on terrain, behaviour, shape and size.

I go out to the Hebrides all the time with Amanda and Chris (two dear friends from Ardnamurchan who I refer to as my Scottish mother and father) in their boat. Out there, I love spotting Storm Petrels.

Once, I was out on the boat with Amanda and I pointed them out.

'I'd never have known that was a Storm Petrel,' she said. 'I always thought they were Manx Shearwaters.'

'Manx Shearwaters do look similar but they're much bigger,' I said. 'A Storm Petrel is only a bit bigger than a sparrow, has webbed feet and basically sits on the sea or does this thing where it holds its wings up in a V-shape while its feet paddle in the water.'

When she first saw one with me she was so excited. And then a few weeks later, I got a call from her saying: 'Hamza, I managed to identify a Storm Petrel, without you!' That's the jackpot for me, giving people the tools to go and find these beautiful creatures themselves. They've flown the nest! When someone gives me a description of a bird based on something I've taught them, it's such an amazing feeling. And what's even more amazing is that once people are that excited about something, they tend to want to tell other people about it. That's what I want this book to be about!

Optics

One of the great things about birding is that you don't need to spend a lot to get involved. I mean, you can just use your eyes! They will help you see quite a few common birds. But if you want to check out some of the more unusual birds around you, or if you're going on holiday, it's really worth getting yourself a pair of binoculars. These don't have to be expensive, unwieldy things. Sharpness is all you need.

You can choose a small, fairly cheap travel pair that will fit in a pocket and you can whip out as and when you need them. Suddenly, you'll be able to zoom in on the plummeting dark shape of a Peregrine Falcon going after a Pigeon, examine the beautiful feathers of a hovering Kestrel, or follow that little Treecreeper silently climbing a tree trunk. Binoculars open you up to a world of possibilities, and the best thing is that world is on your doorstep. You're just looking in more detail. And when you see the breath coming out of a Song Thrush as it sings in the cool morning air, it's quite something. It's almost as if you can see the musical notes appearing!

Binoculars work by taking in light through a lens (called the objective lens), which travels to another lens that magnifies what you see through the eyepiece. Before the image reaches your eyepiece, though, the light needs to travel through prisms, which turn the image you see the right way around. And if the word 'prism' looks a bit frightening and reminds you of sitting in a classroom being told to pay attention while your eyes are glazing over, it just means 'block of glass'. Without them, the image you see would be upside down, and that happens because when light rays travel through a convex lens (a lens where the curve is outwards-facing, as opposed to concave, where the curve faces inwards), they cross over.

There are two main types of binoculars, which are named after the type of prisms used inside. The first type is Porro prism binoculars, which is named after Ignazio Porro, a 19th-century Italian inventor. It involves two prisms, shaped like right-angled triangles (i.e. triangles with one side always upright), positioned alongside each other. This makes the light travel in an S-shaped path towards the eyepiece. And that's why this type of binoculars looks 'stepped' from the outside, because the light doesn't travel in a straight path. The second type is roof prism binoculars, named after the fact that the two roof prisms inside look like the roof of a house. These two prisms are positioned back to back, which means that the light travels in a straight path from the objective lens to the eyepiece. Clever, eh? This means that they can be smaller, slimmer and lighter. It also means they can be a bit more expensive, as the clever prism design is harder to make than the triangular prisms used in Porro prism binoculars. Porro prism binos typically give you a higher-quality image and a slightly clearer picture, because you don't lose as much light. But they are bulkier and typically aren't waterproof. So which is better? Annoyingly, the answer depends on what you're after. My advice is: if you prefer the advantages of roof prisms, get some good ones. But the best thing to do is to try before you buy so you can get an idea of the weight and see how comfortable they feel.

I've had the same pair of Leica Geovid 10x42 magnification binoculars for eight years now, and they're fantastic. Leica are an amazing camera and lens maker from Germany, going back to the 19th century. And when they started making binoculars, they knocked it out of the park. I'm not sponsored by them or anything – they're just that good! Yeah, I've broken bits off and I send them back and they repair them but nothing's gone wrong with the insides yet, touch wood. My Leica pair is a bit fancier because it has a rangefinder, which sends out a light to the place you're pointing at and calculates how far you are away from it and shows you on a little square that pops up in your eyepiece. It also tells you temperature, barometric pressure, and the angle. These kinds of things aren't that useful in amateur birding, but they're actually really useful in my line of work because I have to apply for a licence to photograph Eagles, and you have to tell the authorities how far away your hide is from the nest, and I can do that exactly. I know that my hide is exactly 49 metres away from a White-tailed Eagle nest. The rangefinder's also great when you're working with a couple of people and you're trying to triangulate a bird's position.

My binos are literally on me 24/7 along with my walking stick (I've had that for 12 years), walking boots, laptop and my passport. I took them all with me when I went down to London to do *Strictly Come Dancing*, although, to be fair, I did look a bit weird walking around Wembley with a massive stick. But you never know where you might end up called out on a job at a moment's notice and I need to be able to go straight away. It's happened plenty of times before, if I'm out on a birding trip with some friends, and then I get a call. Can you be at Heathrow in 12 hours, Hamza? Yup!

The other piece of specialised equipment I have is a spotting scope which gives me up to 70x magnification and the clarity is unbelievable. That was the only thing I didn't take along with me when I came down to London for *Strictly*, because I figured I wouldn't have the chance to set it up and have the time to really look at something. I was right!

Whenever I'm out on a dog walk with a friend, it feels like a reconnaissance mission. I can be doing something else, and then a bird will get my attention and I'll recognise that it was doing the same thing yesterday. So I'll go and investigate and realise that it was trying to build a nest. The next day, I'll go past and see it with a twig in its beak and I'll smile to myself because I know exactly what it's up to and where it's going. I make a little note in the Notes section of my phone for birds I've seen (I have one for each year) and then off I go. It just makes everything a lot easier to check out properly if you've got your binos. If you don't, it's OK, but you might just have to be a bit more patient. To start each Note in the right way, I do try and seek out a 'big one' – a slightly more unusual bird. Normally, I can guarantee a Barn Owl, because I know where they roost, so there have been times when I'll be with friends, we'll say 'Happy New Year!' and then we'll creep out to a barn nearby just so people can say the first bird of the year for them was a Barn Owl. But last year I tried that, and the Barn Owls had scarpered! So as soon as it got light, we headed out to the Ardnamurchan Lighthouse. I was still set on seeing a really cool bird. But I literally closed my eyes so I couldn't see any other bird until we were at the lighthouse and I had my binos on.

And then, amazingly, I thought I saw a Little Auk, a black-and-white seabird, only about the size of a Starling, that has these distinctive whirring wingbeats and flies really low over the water's surface. It was a stormy day and it was battling through the wind. I couldn't believe it at first because only a few of them come to the UK, but it was a Little Auk, and my friend and I were both so excited, especially because it was our first bird of the year!

My binos are almost always on a harness I've had for years that I affectionately call my 'man bra' because it hangs on me perfectly, doesn't weigh on my neck and basically looks like I'm wearing a backpack. The harness stops any rain from getting near the bino covers and is designed so that I can crawl along the floor without the binos bouncing around underneath me. They're right next to me when I need them. No, binos and harness are always there. Forgetting them would be like going for a dog walk without a dog lead.

The next thing to think about is what magnification you need. It's not just a case of the higher the magnification, the better, because binos with higher magnification are heavier and trickier to focus. So if you're looking at birds that are moving pretty quickly, they might not be the best bet for you. For everyday birdwatching when you're out and about, 7x or 8x magnification is absolutely fine. You'll see birds on a feeder clearly, foraging at the end of the garden, on that tree over there in the park, flitting about by the river, that sort of thing. They're also a bit more forgiving because they've got a wider field of view, which makes it easier to recognise where exactly you're looking at through the binos when you're trying to locate the bird. They're also better in lower-light conditions.

It's worth investing in higher magnification if you're interested in staying still and watching birds from a hide or want to see birds that are further away from you around coasts, estuaries, large lakes or circling over mountains. Anything that's over about 20 metres away, basically. And if you're in that category, great! You might want to think about a telescope and a tripod. Most of them now have interchangeable eyepieces, allowing you to change the magnification. But you can also buy fixed eyepieces and zoom eyepieces. Magnification-wise, telescopes range from 10x to over 75x depending on how far away you are (and how much you want to spend, because a good telescope will cost upwards of £500, plus the tripod, but it's completely worth it if it brings you joy and you're going to use it a lot). Telescopes can have problems with colour fringing (also known as 'purple ringing' and more technically as chromatic aberration) where objects are ringed with unusual colours, but you can invest in extra-low-dispersion glass (often abbreviated as 'ED') which can solve this issue. It will reward you in the long term because glass never deteriorates. Good glass will stay like that the whole time!

If you're wondering what the figures mean when you look for a pair of binoculars, the first number will be the magnification (e.g. 8 x 32). The second figure is the diameter of the lens. The larger the lens, the brighter the picture you get (because a bigger lens lets more light in). You might also see the letters 'GA' or 'RA', which means that the binoculars are protected by rubber so they can deal with some bumps and shocks, which will happen at some point, I guarantee! They're also a bit easier to grip. The letter 'B' means that the binoculars have push-down or twist-down eye cups to suit you if you usually wear glasses so you can see the full image.

If you are going to be birding around sploshing water or in the rain, you'll want to go for waterproof binoculars, which are both completely sealed and filled with nitrogen rather than regular air, which stops the lenses fogging up and prevents dust and dirt from getting in.

HABITATS

CITIES, PARKS AND GARDENS

Cities are actually great places to look for wildlife because you don't have to go far to find something, the public transport links are usually good and what you do find will often surprise you. One of the best places to look for the fastest bird in the world – the Peregrine Falcon – is around skyscrapers in cities. And why's that? They love hunting Pigeons. And where are Pigeons plentiful? Big cities! It always surprises people to learn that there are breeding pairs of Peregrine Falcons in most major cities in Europe including London (there are around 30 pairs in London), Paris, Brussels, Amsterdam, Berlin, Madrid, Rome, Warsaw and now Copenhagen. At first glance though, when they're in level flight, it's easy to mistake them for pigeons. They both have bulky, strong bodies, short tails, are mainly grey, and fly in a similar way. But once you can tell the difference, your daily commute might just become a whole lot more interesting!

Try and use all your senses (well, except taste, maybe!) and go out for a walk as much as you can. Keep your eyes and ears open and enjoy it, and next time you'll see something really cool. If you sit and wait in a garden or park, there's much more bird life about than you think. It's not just Pigeons, House Sparrows, Magpies and Starlings. You might catch sight of a Song Thrush, a Jay or a Great Spotted Woodpecker. In summer, you'll hear groups of screaming Swifts chasing each other at breakneck speed in between buildings. And if you listen out, you'll hear Wrens and maybe even the smallest European bird, the stunning Goldcrest. And if you put out a garden feeder, you'll find you're attracting Robins, Blue Tits, Great Tits and slightly less familiar but beautiful garden birds like Goldfinches and Chaffinches.

BLACKBIRD

Scientific name: *Turdus merula*

Conservation status (UK/Europe): Green/Secure

In three words: Dark, yellow-beaked songster

Look out for them: Gobbling worms on a lawn; singing from tall trees and chimney pots at dawn and dusk

How easy it is to see them: Really Easy, and if you can't see them, you'll hear them

Blackbirds have got a lot of character and they're such beautiful singers. You'll see and hear them, happy as anything as dusk approaches, singing from chimney pots or tall trees. Their song is a loud, musical, melodious warbling that starts with beautiful fluted notes and then kind of collapses into a slightly unmusical squeak, like it's run out of breath. But that's far from the only sound they make. You'll also have heard their panicky alarm call when they've been disturbed by something, calling as they fly low and fast away from whatever has upset them. And during the day, Blackbirds can be heard making a call that sounds a bit like 'chuck-chuck'. That's just for a chit-chat with their neighbours. But the song they sing during the night is lonesome and mournful and because there are no other sounds, it just travels far and wide.

In the country, if you hear a Blackbird going completely nuts with loud, high-pitched alarm calls near the end of the night (or even during the night), I guarantee you there'll be a Tawny Owl nearby in a tree probably hidden in the ivy with its eyes closed. So if you hear something like that and you scan your environment slowly and patiently, you'll find the hidden source of the commotion. And if something like that happens, I know that this is where the Tawny Owl likes to hunt from, so I'll set up my camera so I can capture it. I feel like the Blackbirds are saying to me 'Help me, human. If I try and roost on that tree that I usually like, I'm going to get eaten by that Tawny Owl who's hiding in the ivy! Can you not see it? I can see it and we better both back up!' I know that's anthropomorphising, but we know when a bird is stressed. Blackbirds rely a lot on their eyesight and when the sun goes down and they haven't got to their roost place yet (where they feel nice and safe and comfortable), they're always a bit nervous.

Blackbirds have adapted amazingly well to all environments, except mountains. Amazingly, in cities, they've developed a higher pitch to sing at that's easier to hear amid the low-frequency rumble of traffic. They also sing earlier in towns than in the countryside and sing louder so their song travels further. There's also evidence that Blackbird song gets more complicated as they get older because they're really good learners and mimics, not just of Blackbirds and other birds, but also the noises we make and the machines we use. So the more they learn, the more they have to mimic and the more varied their song gets. Who says you can't teach an old bird new tricks?

Females are dark brown with streaks and spots visible on their breasts. They have duller, yellowy-brown beaks, don't have the yellow eye ring that the male has and are a bit bigger than males. Both males and females are territorial, defending their breeding grounds fiercely. You're most likely to see them running across a garden, digging up a worm and then darting for cover.

Dave Leech, who works for the British Trust for Ornithology (BTO) set up the Holt Blackbird Project in 2007 to study Blackbirds in his parents' garden in Norfolk and discovered some pretty fascinating stuff. If you think you're seeing the same Blackbird in your garden every day, you're probably wrong! Dave recorded 74 different Blackbirds visiting the garden during the breeding season in just one day.

GOLDCREST (AND FIRECREST)

Scientific name: *Regulus regulus*
Conservation status (UK/Europe): Green/Least Concern
In three words: Tiny, active, beautiful
Look out for: Golden crest; flitting about in conifer trees catching insects
How easy it is to see them: Challenging – they're very small and move about a lot

These two are little garden gems. And I mean 'little' – the Goldcrest is around 4.5 grams, a little over the weight of a 20p coin, while the Firecrest is more like 5–7 grams, so roughly the same weight as a 10p piece. Incredibly, despite being that tiny, they still manage to look plump when you see one, partly because they have a 'no-neck' look. They're not common garden birds and they won't visit feeders but they are keen on conifer trees, which they'll flit about searching for insects. You'll need to be patient because they can be tricky to spot, being both tiny and never staying still for long enough! You'll hear them before you see them, and when you do, get the binoculars ready because you don't want to miss the patch on their crowns. It's always a thrill when the smallest birds in the UK (and Europe) have decided to visit your place and you catch them in your binoculars for long enough to see that incredible crown.

Both Goldcrests and Firecrests look similar, but they have different head markings, both of which are beautiful. The Goldcrest has a yellow stripe that runs almost from the beak to the back of its head, bordered by two black stripes. You can tell the male apart from the female because the yellow stripe has an orange centre. When they're displaying to attract a female (or just annoyed about something!), they raise and spread out their crests and bow their heads, so you can get a proper look at what is an amazing hairstyle. When they're not displaying, the crest can be difficult to spot, but if you see an ordinary-looking tiny green-and-grey bird in a conifer, hang around and take a second look!

Although they're found in the same kind of trees looking for the same kind of food, you're more likely to see a Goldcrest, which is a permanent resident all over the UK (except for a few places in mostly north-west Scotland) and throughout most of France, Germany, Switzerland, Poland, Denmark, the Czech Republic, most of Norway, the southern part of Sweden and Finland and western Russia. The Firecrest does breed in the UK (it's more common in western and central Europe) but only in a few areas of southern and eastern England. You're more likely to see it in winter in southern and south-east England and Wales. Sometimes they make surprise and very welcome appearances in gardens.

Goldcrests love conifers, and picking insects and spiders out from between pine needles with their short, sharp bills. These guys never sit still and are always flitting about. You might even see them hovering to catch an insect, which is pretty impressive. They have this really high-pitched, slightly screechy call that sounds like 'zee, zee, zee, zee, zee' and their song is similar, sounding more like 'dee dullee dee dullee'.

Sometimes in late August, September and October, they migrate in huge numbers from Scandinavia to the east coast of the UK, where you might find them in bushes and sometimes gardens. Its scientific name is *Regulus regulus*, which comes from the Latin word *Rex* meaning 'king', which is thought to come from the crown on its head.

Like the Goldcrest, the Firecrest flits about from tree to tree (typically conifers) looking for insects, spiders and larvae, but it does like to forage lower down in trees, scrub and bushes than Goldcrests. You can tell them apart thanks to the Firecrest's striking white stripe above its eye and the black band that runs through the eye and below it. Its markings are a bit brighter and it's a little less plump-looking.

MAGPIE

Scientific name: *Pica pica*

Conservation status (UK/Europe): Green/Secure

In three words: Loud, confident, intelligent

Look out for: Magpie pairs – if you see one, there's almost always another close by; those amazing blues and greens on its wings and tail

How easy it is to see them: Really Easy

Everyone knows what a Magpie looks like, so you won't need any help there. But I do want to tell you a thing or two about these incredible birds, because they do get a bit of bad press. Maybe it's because they're common, noisy, pretty brazen, sound like they're laughing at you, are thought to steal things, or because seeing one on its own is traditionally unlucky. Or maybe all of these reasons! But hear me out.

The first thing is their tail. It just looks black from afar, but if you catch it in the right light, it shimmers with glossy greens, bronzes and purple near the tip. The wing feathers, head and neck are similar, but often have flashes of shimmering greens and blues. The tail is also so long that it's the same length as a Magpie's body. And when it's held open, you realise that it's a beautiful diamond-shape. So why is it so long? It could be something to do with being able to make quick turns. Or it could be related to mating. A study in 1997 showed that Magpies with broken and damaged tails paired up later than those without damaged tails. Those with really broken tails didn't mate at all. So it seems like Magpies rate each other based on the quality of their tails. Their tails do grow back, though, in a couple of months, in case you're feeling sorry for them!

Magpies are among the most intelligent birds in the world. They might even *be* the most intelligent. There's a famous experiment called the Mirror Test, first carried out in the early 1970s in the US to see if animals can recognise themselves in a mirror. You could probably guess some of the species who passed it – great apes (chimps, gorillas, orangutans and bonobos), bottlenose dolphins, orcas, Asian elephants...and the Magpie. Yup, that's right, the first non-mammal to pass this test is the Magpie. The test involved putting a single sticker on their throats (a place beyond their normal field of vision) and then placing them in a large box with mirrors around the outside. Some of the stickers were brightly coloured, and others were black. Well, two out of the five Magpies with the brightly coloured stickers began trying to remove the stickers with their bills and feet, while the Magpies with the invisible black stickers didn't react. So the ones with the brightly coloured stickers knew they were looking at themselves in the mirror.

Magpies weren't always called Magpies. Until the 17th century, they were actually just called 'Pies'! I always thought that the 'pie' was a short version of 'pied' meaning black and white, like with the Pied Wagtail, but it's not quite true. I've learned a lot writing this book! 'Pied' was actually used to describe birds that resembled a Magpie (or 'Pie' as it would have been then). But that doesn't explain where 'pie' comes from. Well, it seems that 'pie' might originate with 'pi' meaning 'pointed' in reference to the shape of its tail or possibly its beak. The 'Mag' part of the word we do know for sure, though.

And we can blame the patriarchy for this one. Mag is short for Margaret, and this name was used in English slang for characteristics 'associated' with women, like chattering. So the Magpie is another candidate for renaming, I'd say!

Time for a bit of myth debunking. It seems that Magpies don't steal shiny things. A study in 2014 by scientists at Exeter University showed that they're actually quite nervous around shiny objects. Magpies were offered piles of nuts, which were placed close to a pile of shiny objects. Out of 64 tests, Magpies only picked up a shiny object twice, and dropped it straight away each time! So while you do hear the occasional story about an engagement ring found in a Magpie's nest, these really are one-off tales. It wouldn't be a news item if it was any other bird but because they've become associated with shiny things, they're always carrying around the bad press!

PEREGRINE FALCON

Scientific name: *Falco peregrinus*

Conservation status (UK/Europe): Green/Secure

In three words: Powerful, patient, adaptable

Listen/look out for: Repeated one-note scream; dark head with a curved 'moustache' under the eyes; thick, barred chest

How easy it is to see them: Hard – you'll need binoculars; look out for ledges on the top of tall buildings; listen out for the scream

Birds of prey have a tough life. I sometimes feel sorry for them because they're always getting mobbed by Crows or constantly monitored by other birds. It's like they're villains, but I see them completely differently. They're the lords of the skies, making the judgement calls that affect the rest of the food chain. There's a big Carlsberg brewery near my parents' house in Northampton with its bright neon-green sign. I was walking by one day and heard what sounded like the distinctive peeping call of a Peregrine Falcon, but I thought I must be mistaken. But then I saw one fly by and land directly on the sign. I rushed back home, grabbed my binoculars and came back. And to my surprise, there was not one but a pair of Peregrines. They were using the sign as a roost, sleeping there for most of the evening, but also to hunt from. I saw the female take down a Pigeon and come back to the roost with it. It was amazing and slightly surreal to see all this in the town centre of Northampton. Since humans have started building factories, big blocks of flats and skyscrapers, birds have been using the ledges, roofs and balconies as artificial cliff edges – the perfect habitat to roost and hunt from.

One thing that identifies a Peregrine Falcon is the distinctive black, slightly curved 'moustache' that runs under its eye. It looks a bit like an upside-down shark's fin. In fact, the whole look of a Peregrine's head reminds me of a medieval executioner's mask. The name

'Peregrine' is derived from a Latin word that means 'coming from abroad'. The word 'peregrine' came to mean 'pilgrim' or 'wandering' because their nests were often difficult to access, being on high ledges or cliffs. This was a problem for falconers in medieval times, so they were forced to seize them on their first flight (or pilgrimage) from the nest.

Peregrines are well known for being the fastest birds in the world. They reach incredible speeds, thanks to their hunting technique of flying to high altitudes, then attacking birds on the wing in a fast, controlled dive. It's known as stooping, and it isn't unique to Peregrines, but the speed they generate is. They can reach speeds of well over 200mph (the fastest was recorded as 242mph, but this was a trained Peregrine called 'Frightful' who was released from a plane at a height of 17,000 feet, which is higher than they would usually attack from, so she had a bit of an unfair advantage. It's a bit like a sprinter breaking the 100-metre world record while pushed along by a 70mph tail wind!).

I've seen a few in London. Just sitting in a hotel room by the river with office blocks and skyscrapers on the other side I've seen them fly by chasing Pigeons. Many skyscrapers across Europe and the US will have had Peregrines roosting on them at some point. Skyscrapers are basically artificial cliffs and Peregrines are historically cliff-dwellers who hunt seabirds or Pigeons that fly past but because of the environment we've built, they've moved in naturally to take advantage of the food. Pigeons are basically fast food for a Peregrine – there's always one around whenever you want it! It's a kind of accidental conservation success story. If we were all only a couple of floors off the ground, like we were during the Industrial Revolution, Peregrines would be happily in their cliffs. They need the height, to give them the vantage point over other birds and also to let gravity do some of the work while they hunt.

REDWING

Scientific name: *Turdus iliacus*

Conservation status (UK/Europe): Amber/Near Threatened

In three words: Visiting winter berry-fiend!

Look out for: A Blackbird-sized thrush with red patches under the wings

How easy it is to see them: (Winter only): Challenging – look out for them near berry bushes and in fields in flocks with other thrushes

It's always a special moment hearing these guys at the beginning of autumn making their beautiful 'tseep tseep' calls in the night. One year, I think I was on the way back from the pub and I ended up just standing there, closing my eyes and listening to them fly over my head! They're sociable birds and they migrate in large flocks during the night, coming from Iceland and the Faroe Islands. But the first you know about it, you suddenly hear something that sounds a bit like a Blackbird, but then you hear another, then another and another, and I know it's the Redwings migrating south. It's a bit of an honour living in one of the first patches of land Redwings will fly over on their long journey. Nearly 700,000 of them will travel over here in October and November before leaving again in March and April.

Look out for them in your local park or hedges in the countryside. They absolutely love berries, especially hawthorn and rowan, so if there's a bush nearby, you'll probably see one at some point adding a bit of colour to a winter's day. A Redwing is a really exciting bird to see the first time because you only see them for part of the year and they've travelled a long way to get here. At first glance, they look like Song Thrushes, but what sets them apart is the orange-red patches on their sides and under their wings that almost looks like they've spent too long outside and have gone a bit rusty. They've also got a clear white eyestripe above their eyes that extends to the back of their head. They're also a bit smaller and often travel in flocks, but the giveaway will be where you see them. If you see a thrush on a berry bush in winter, it might well be a Redwing. They don't tend to visit gardens that often unless you have a berry bush, or unless you put some bits of broken apple and pear on your lawn – perfect for a cold, hungry Redwing!

Redwings' love of berries made them the subject of a study to see exactly how they locate them. We know that birds, unlike humans, can see ultraviolet (UV) light, but it wasn't understood until 1999 that UV light helps them find their food. It turns out that the waxy coatings of blue, black and violet berries, like bilberries, reflect UV light, so they stand out to a Redwing. It's a similar thing to bumblebees being guided towards certain flowers, which advertise themselves with UV areas of their petals that look just like little landing strips to a bee.

RING-NECKED PARAKEET

Scientific name: *Psittacula krameri*

Conservation status (UK/Europe): Introduced/Not Evaluated

In three words: Loud, sociable, green

Listen/Look out for: A very noisy and squeaky commotion from a group in a city park; long green tail; red, hooked beak

How easy it is to see them: Fairly Easy, in major western European cities

Just before I joined *Strictly Come Dancing*, I was in London. I say that like it was no big deal, but as I mentioned, it was actually the first time I'd really been to London. And one of the first things I remember is seeing four or five long green tails flashing by, banking like fighter jets, and hearing something I'd never heard before. It sounded a bit like a high-pitched laugh mixed with the squeak of a dog toy and I thought, *those can't be parakeets, can they?* And then lo and behold, I looked it up and found out they were Ring-tailed Parakeets. And then I find out that there are all sorts of urban legends flying about how these incredible birds ended up in London. The best is probably the one about Jimi Hendrix supposedly releasing a pair of them on Carnaby Street in the 1960s. And then there's the one about a bunch of Parakeets (or 'chatter' if we're being strictly accurate on the collective nouns) escaping from the set of *The African Queen* in the 1950s, and the tall tale about the plane crashing into the aviary roof of Syon Park in west London and their prized parakeets escaping.

The truth is slightly less exciting but no less amazing.

They became really popular pets, especially in London after the Second World War, and after a lot of releases and escapes, they've thrived here. That's probably because the climate here isn't that different from the parts of northern India and Pakistan where they originally come from. So these beautiful creatures are second- and third-generation migrants, if you think about it!

You can find them in and around London, Surrey, Kent and Sussex, where they live year-round. It's not just the UK that they've settled in, though. There have been similar releases and escapes in other cities around Europe, like Brussels, Amsterdam, Paris, Rome, Barcelona and Cologne. But it's not all been plain sailing for the Parakeets, because they've found themselves on the menu for birds of prey that have adapted well to cities and parks. To be fair, they are bright green, fly high and make a lot of noise, so they're ideal for Peregrine Falcons, who have been filmed taking them back to their roosts. But there are also Tawny Owls in London's parks, who are perching high up in trees, doing their camouflage thing and waiting for parakeets to land on a nearby tree lower down than the Tawny, who then swoops down completely silently to ambush them.

They mainly nest in trees in tree holes made by Woodpeckers in parks and form large flocks that have a habit of making their presence known! They're resourceful birds and will come to garden feeders, especially in winter when the supply of fruit, nuts, seeds and berries is lower and they need to keep their energy levels up to cope with the cold.

ROCK DOVE (AND FERAL PIGEON)

Scientific name: *Columba livia domestica*

Conservation status (UK/Europe): Green/Secure

In three words: Confident, sociable, ground-dweller

Look out for: Groups in city centres, flocks either in the air or perched on building ledges; shimmering purples and greens on their necks; courtship ritual involving the male bowing, cooing, puffing out the chest and fanning its tail

How easy it is to see them: Really Easy

The Rock Dove is the wild ancestor of the Feral Pigeon and is now only found in remote, rocky areas of Scotland and Northern Ireland. The domesticated version – the Feral Pigeon – is the one you can see pretty much everywhere. The Woodpigeon is a similar-looking bird, but is quite a bit fatter and has distinctive white wing patches in flight and you won't find it in city centres in the same way as a Feral Pigeon. People often hate feral pigeons and call them 'rats of the sky' and things like that. But most of it is because we see them all the time and have got used to them, so we don't take the time to recognise how extraordinary they are. It's a bit like when you go to a big city abroad and are really excited to see a bird you've never seen before, but you realise that people are looking at you strangely because they're wondering why you're staring at something so common. Why's that guy standing there staring at a Pigeon? So, the next time you see one, try to imagine it's the first you've ever seen. You might see them in a new light. They've got a ring of metallic, shiny feathers on their necks that blends into an iridescent purple on their breast. They've got two black wingstripes on each wing and most can fly at an impressive 50–60mph. One was even flashed by a speed camera in Germany in 2019, flying 7.5mph above the residential speed limit!

You might have seen their funny courtship ritual, where the male puffs up his neck feathers, fans its tail, struts, bows and walks quickly over and around the female while making a series of coos. Also, when they take off, you'll hear a cracking sound, which happens when the tips of both wings hit each other at the top of the upstroke.

They're descendants of the Domestic Pigeon (*Columbia livia domestica*), which was the first bird humans domesticated, at least 5,000 years ago. Trained Domestic Pigeons are pretty incredible animals, with remarkable navigational abilities, which we still don't fully understand. We know that they use visual landmarks like roads and rivers and they do seem to respond to the Earth's magnetic field to some extent but how they do this remains a mystery. It's possible they navigate using low-frequency sound (or infrasound) to make a kind of acoustic map of home. This theory came about when John Hagstrum, a geologist at the US Geological Survey, discovered that racing pigeons were getting lost just as Concorde was flying over the speed of sound, which creates shockwaves and a thunderous sound known as a sonic boom. He showed that Pigeons can recognise the low-frequency rumble associated with a particular area, which acts like a homing beacon. That's the best theory I've heard, anyway!

STARLING

Scientific name: *Sturnus vulgaris*

Conservation status (UK/Europe): Red/Near Threatened

In three words: Cheeky, confident, vocal

Look out for: Large groups (murmurations) moving across the sky as one towards dusk in winter; beautiful chevrons on its breast

How easy it is to see them: Really Easy

I've included the Starling because it's one of the most underrated birds there is. Everyone sees them and kind of forgets them, but if you look closely at a Starling, you'll see that their feathers shimmer with iridescent greens, blues, purples, even a touch of copper. And the little white blotches on their breasts are more intricate than that – they're little chevrons or love-heart shapes, depending on how you want to look at life! Starlings are incredible mimics too, able to incorporate all sorts of different sounds, including other animal calls into their own. Their range of vocalizations is just amazing: chattering, rattling, whistling, clicking, to name just four types.

Starlings are well known for forming great flocks called murmurations in November (sometimes as early as September though) that dance across the sky in shape-shifting clouds before they roost together for the night. They begin towards dusk with more and more birds reuniting with their flock near their roost sites. Sometimes their numbers can reach hundreds of thousands. What fascinates me is which Starling decides 'That's all, folks!' and signals those around it to make for the roost. A study published in 2013 discovered that each Starling monitors the movements of the seven birds closest to it and coordinates its behaviour with them. And every group of seven is attached to other groups of seven. We know that Starlings' reaction and processing speed is so much faster than ours, but we're not sure how they can produce such incredible collective responses. And to be honest, we're still not entirely sure why they form murmurations. Not even Attenborough knows! It could be a defence mechanism to confuse and put off predators. It could be to keep warm. There is strength in numbers, after all. Some of the best places to see them are over piers, like the Palace Pier and West Pier in Brighton, the Royal Pier in Aberystwyth and the North Pier in Blackpool. The Albert Bridge in Belfast and Gretna Green, in Dumfries and Galloway also play host to spectacular murmurations. We're spoiled for choice.

Although it's called the Common Starling, it's also known as the European Starling in North America. And that's because Starlings were introduced there in the 19th century. Sixty of them were released in New York's Central Park by a chap called Eugene Schieffelin in 1890 in the hope that they would breed, which they certainly did (!) given that they now number over 200 million there. Schieffelin was an eccentric ornithologist and president of something called the American Acclimatization Society, a group who wanted to introduce various plants and animals to North America. The story goes that he was a big Shakespeare fan and wanted to introduce all the birds that appear in the works of Shakespeare. It's almost certainly an urban legend, but it shouldn't get in the way of a good story! Starlings weren't the only bird species released in Central Park in the 19th century, though. House Sparrows, Blackbirds, Chaffinches, Skylarks and Nightingales were also set free, but only the Sparrows took off, so to speak.

Although they're listed on the Global Invasive Species Database, which is administered by the IUCN (the International Union for Conservation of Nature), Starlings are actually on the Red List in the UK, the list of birds that need our help. And that surprises people because while they seem quite common, their numbers have dropped by two-thirds in the past 25 years in the UK.

Starlings have a special place in my heart. There's a little hole in one of the fascia boards of my house in Scotland. We get strong Atlantic winds here and it's been degrading the wood. I'm slowly getting things fixed, but a group of Starlings has started nesting in the hole in summer so I don't really want to fix it up because it feels like some beautiful friends are coming back each year to visit me! I love hearing the sounds get louder and louder in the three weeks that follow, and then it goes completely quiet and I realise that the chicks have fledged. There's always a touch of sadness about that moment but it's outweighed by the joy I feel that another group of Starlings are out there living their lives. It's such a lovely feeling that my home is home to other animals. Sometimes it's much better for the nature around you to leave a manageable hole here or there, an unmowed area of your lawn, a pile of logs to encourage animals to join you in the place you love.

The last thing to say is that if you've been converted and see the Starling in a new light, some of the other members of the Starling family are even more stunning. The Chestnut-bellied Starling and the Greater Blue-eared Starling were birds I used to see in Sudan, and wow! And then there's the Emerald Starling and the Superb Starling, also native to Africa, and the Golden Myna, all of which have to be seen to be believed. Enjoy!

SWIFT

Scientific name: *Apus apus*

Conservation status (UK/Europe): Red/Near Threatened

In three words: Fast, aerobatic screamers

Look out for: Crescent-like wings; short, forked tail; seriously agile, rapid flight

How easy it is to see them: (Summer only): Fairly Easy – look for them zooming around rooftops chasing each other

If you've ever wondered what that passing screaming sound is towards dusk on summer evenings as you look up at the sky, it's a group of Swifts performing high-speed aerobatic stunts. You might be able to catch a glimpse of several dark shapes with pale throats darting this way and that among the rooftops of buildings in towns and cities (among other places) sometimes banking sharply past some sort of invisible marker like they're competing in the Red Bull Air Race. These are known as 'screaming parties' and it might not come as a surprise that the collective noun for a group of Swifts is a scream! When I was living with my parents in Northampton, I used to love the moment when you can hear the first Swifts arrive. It meant that summer's on the way! I remember being on holiday in Italy, where the buildings are tall and narrow and people hang their washing on lines high up. I've seen Swifts fly above, below and sometimes through these washing lines! You can just about hear the screams just before they appear and they always sound like they're having such a great time.

The Common Swift is so swift that it's actually thought to be the fastest bird in the world in level flight, achieving speeds of up to 69.3mph. The related White-throated Needletail is suspected to fly faster, but the methods used to record its speed haven't been published, so it remains a rumour. The White-throated Needletail is an Asian bird, but it is a rare traveller to the UK.

Amazingly, one was spotted by a group of birders on a ship heading from the Netherlands to Norway off the coast of Caithness in June 2022; even more incredibly, the Needletail tried to land on the metal wall at the back of the bridge of the ship, but lost its grip and fell to the ship's deck with its wings spread. Happily, it wasn't injured and one of the birders, Christopher Gourard, helped it back into the sky. Lucky it landed on a ship full of birders!

Common Swifts are incredible flyers, and they're perfectly designed for a life on the wing, with their long, crescent-shaped wings and sharply forked tails. And that's just as well because Swifts hardly ever use their feet. In 2016, it was finally proven that the Common Swift flies non-stop for ten months of the year. That sounds hard to believe, I know, but they really do everything in the air – eating, sleeping, even mating! They only land to build their nests, which are mostly in crevices in buildings. It's possible that juvenile Swifts spend even longer in the air without landing because they only breed when they're three to four years old, but it hasn't been conclusively proved yet.

Common Swifts aren't just amazing sprinters, though; they're also amazing long-distance migrants. The birds that are screaming around your chimney pots, who weigh about the same as two AA batteries, have travelled from the lower half of Africa. That's around a 6,000-mile journey, without stopping, remember, and they can only do this because they're so good at catching insects in flight, which gives them the energy to keep flying.

Their scientific name, *Apus apus*, comes from an Ancient Greek word that translates as 'without foot' because it was a common belief that they don't have feet. And it's not a surprise that they ended up with that name, given that you can't see their tiny feet and legs when they're flying. Well, they do have feet, with four forward-facing, very strong toes and curved, sharply pointed claws that are designed to cling to cliffs and walls. That's why, in Germany, they're called *Mauersegler*, which means 'wall-glider'. It's often said that a Swift is doomed if its feet touch the ground, which is actually a myth. Their wings are very powerful and adult Swifts can usually take off. It's if they land on something that isn't a level surface, that they can get into trouble, like boggy ground or long grass or if their wings haven't got enough room to flap (as with the ship full of birders).

Sadly, these incredible birds are declining rapidly in the UK. Between 1995 and 2015, their numbers dropped by over 50 per cent. This is thought to be partly because modern buildings don't tend to have that many crevices and holes in them, which they need to build their nests in. A lot of birds need these places to survive, which is one reason I haven't fixed my fascia boards connecting to my roof! One solution, which is already making a difference is an artificial nest brick called a 'swift brick' that either replaces an existing brick in an old wall or is incorporated into a new wall. It's a rectangular, hollow box made from a mixture of concrete and wood or stone and doesn't affect your home's insulation. From the outside of the house you can see the oval-shaped entry hole, and hopefully, a Swift approaching it at ridiculous speed before landing perfectly! In fact, in some towns and cities, installing swift bricks has become a compulsory condition for new property developments. And that's the kind of thing that makes me very happy.

There are two other species that look similar to Swifts: Swallows and House Martins. Swifts are brown all over with the pale throat patch, and have really long, scythe-like wings. Swallows are cream or slightly pinky coloured underneath, dark around the throat and have long tail 'streamers' – one outermost feather on each side of the tail that extends really far back – and shorter wings than the Swift. A House Martin is glossy blue-black above, like the Swallow, but it's completely white below, including its rump. It has a black head, but unlike the Swallow, it has a white throat and no red on its forehead.

WOODS

British and European woods are home to some of the finest and most distinctive vocalists in the bird world, like the beautifully clear, loud and insistent song of the Song Thrush and the crazy cackle of a Green Woodpecker. And then you've got the less visible birds that give away their presence with their calls towards dusk and during the night, like the haunting hooting you get from territorial male Tawny Owls and the bewitching song of the elusive Nightingale. There's always something going on in a wood!

When you're walking through a wood, the birds will know you're there. That's why it might seem really quiet; but if you stay still and wait, you'll be rewarded. But it's also about what to watch out for and listen for. Woodland birds each like specific parts of trees. Great Spotted Woodpeckers can be quite shy in woods and often move around a tree trunk so that they're on the side not facing you! Look out for little camouflaged Treecreepers moving up tree trunks using their incredibly strong toes (with curved claws) and stiff tails, while brightly coloured Nuthatches scurry down them headfirst. A lot of woodland birds nest in holes of different sizes in trees, like Tawny Owls, Great Spotted and Green Woodpeckers, Nuthatches and Great Tits, so keep a look out for activity around any sort of cavity in a tree trunk. Song Thrushes like to sing from prominent branches high up so their song carries as far as possible. Bullfinches love budding fruit trees, Mistle Thrushes adore mistletoe berries and Nightingales like hiding in dense cover low down. I've still never actually ever seen a Nightingale, believe it or not (!) but their song is one of the most incredible things in the animal kingdom.

I could have included about fifty birds in this section, but I've gone for eight of my absolute favourites. Some of these guys you'll be able to see all year round, a couple are summer migrants, only appearing here when it gets warmer, and one – the Wryneck – is a rare visitor which comes out with some of the most extraordinary behaviour of any animal in the world.

BULLFINCH

Scientific name: *Pyrrhula pyrrhula*

Conservation status (UK/Europe): Amber/Secure

In four words: Brightly coloured, shy, chunky

Look out for: Rosy-red breast (greyish-brown in female), black cap and white bum

How easy it is to see them: Challenging – look near the top of budding fruit trees in spring

With their bright pinky red undersides and black hood-like caps, these guys are the jewels of the hedgerows. You'd think the Bullfinch would be as flamboyant as it looks but they're actually shy and quiet birds, disappearing quickly into cover if they've been disturbed, so catching sight of one is a treat. Sometimes all you get is a bright white bum that matches neatly with the bright white stripes on their wings, but that's enough to give it away. Females are less colourful than males, with more of a greyish-brown underside but still with the black hood, white bum and wingstripes.

Bullfinches aren't that keen on bird tables but they can be persuaded to go for hanging seed feeders, so you might be able to attract them to your garden. What these guys love more than anything is fruit trees, so if you've got them in your garden, then you might well find a Bullfinch around. Fruit trees in woodland and hedgerows are their favourite spots, nibbling the apple, cherry, ash, hawthorn and blackthorn buds. Unfortunately, this love of the buds on fruit trees has made Bullfinches really unpopular with farmers, commercial fruit-growers and even Henry VIII, who, labelled them as vermin and put a princely one penny bounty on their heads for their 'criminal attacks' on fruit trees. The reputation for being an orchard pest has meant they've been persecuted since the days of the Tudors. It's why you sometimes see what look like random plastic bags wrapped around fruit trees!

The Bullfinch is thought to get its name from its similarity to a bull, with its chunky head, stocky body and neckless appearance, giving it a kind of front-heavy look. Well, that's the most popular theory, anyway. Although, Francis Orpen Morris, the renowned 19th-century reverend/naturalist and author, thought differently, suggesting that 'Bullfinch' is a corruption of 'Budfinch'. And then there's the theory that it might be a shortened form of 'Bullace', the Tudor name for a wild plum tree. Take your pick!

Finches have specialised bills that are shaped to suit the food they eat. A Hawfinch has this huge conical bill with a serrated lining, so it can hold and crack fruit stones. A Bullfinch has a much stubbier, rounded black bill, which is ideal for taking off the outer coats of seeds. They seem to be quite particular in what kind of insects, seeds and berries they go for, which can mean they need to travel a fair distance from home. But not to worry – they've adapted special sacs in the bottom of their mouths to store food while they're foraging. Genius, and they're the only finches to have developed them.

As for its song, it's been likened to a squeaky wheelbarrow (!), but that doesn't do justice to a Bullfinch's singing ability. They actually have amazing memories and can learn entire fluted or whistled melodies. That made Bullfinches very popular caged birds in the 19th century and they'd be taught to sing tunes like 'God Save the

Queen' and 'Yankee Doodle Dandy'. They'd actually sing the songs better than their human teachers, because there wouldn't be any pausing for breath or anything like that.

Although Bullfinch numbers fell sharply in the 1970s and continued to fall until around 2000, they seem to be increasing slowly again, which is amazing. And hopefully that will keep rising until they're taken off the Amber List, which highlights UK birds of moderate concern. Bullfinches are quite widespread, found in all areas of the UK except the far north of Scotland – you just need to know where to look. Be patient, and you'll be rewarded!

GREAT SPOTTED WOODPECKER

Scientific name: *Dendrocopos major*

Conservation status (UK/Europe): Green/Secure

In three words: Black-and-white, Blackbird-sized, tree-dweller

Listen/look out for: Short, squeaky, repeated 'chip' or 'chik' call; short drumming sound (in spring); bouncy flight pattern

How easy it is to see them: Fairly Easy if you're patient and keep looking up towards the tops of thick, tall trees; or load up a feeder with peanuts!

This is your slightly more exotic garden bird. I say 'garden' bird, but you'll find them across all sorts of habitats involving trees, so think garden, parks and deciduous and coniferous woodland. It's just that more exciting when they choose to visit your garden! They love garden feeders loaded with peanuts in particular.

The Great Spotted Woodpecker is the most numerous and widely distributed woodpecker in Europe, although you won't find them in parts of northern Scotland and they've only relatively recently made it over to Ireland, but only to the east coast.

They're actually only about the same size as a Blackbird, but they stand out with their distinctive and dapper black-and-white pattern. You can identify a male from the bright little red patch on the nape of its neck; both males and female have a scarlet red belly and bum, but it's more pinkish in young woodpeckers, who also have a red cap. You might be able to hear a Great Spotted Woodpecker announce itself with its loud, clear and often repeated 'chip' call that reminds me a bit of a squeaky dog toy. Either that or the short, sharp drumming sound it makes in springtime while it drills into a tree, which only lasts about a second each time. It doesn't just do this to dig out insects or excavate holes to nest in. It also does it to tell other rivals *this is my patch, so back off*!

They're pretty incredible creatures, Woodpeckers. They've got everything they need right in front of them to eat, attract a mate and build a home. Not many of us can say that! A Great Spotted Woodpecker uses a number of techniques to feed: probing, gleaning, tapping and digging. It's also learned to find, use and maintain 'anvils' to give it a bit of help cracking nuts and breaking open seeds from pine and other conifer cones. It uses anvils of different shapes and sizes depending on the size of the cone it needs to wedge in place. Clever stuff.

But my favourite thing about Great Spotted Woodpeckers is the way they fly. They look like little torpedoes, flapping for a few beats and then gliding, giving this kind of bouncy looking flight pattern. And then it lands upright, always near the top of a tree.

The Great Spotted Woodpecker does have a more sinister side, though. In spring, they sometimes eat the eggs and chicks of young, smaller birds that nest in holes in trees and will even enlarge the opening to a nest or a nestbox to access it. It does have the tools of the trade, after all. You can buy things like metal plates to reinforce the nest holes, but Great Spotted Woodpeckers are smart and will sometimes just start pecking another hole! When I think about something like that, I try and remember that birds like Blue Tits have up to 12 eggs, and they do that precisely because some are going to be lost to predators, but not all of them are going to be taken by a Woodpecker.

It's not until you've actually held a Woodpecker that you realise quite how stiff their tail feathers are. They use them kind of like a third leg to help stabilise them when they're drilling into tree bark. It's the same as a digger on a building site using its hydraulic stabilisers as well as its wheels to anchor it in place. That's not the most amazing thing about a Woodpecker, though. They can drum into wood up to 22 times a second, which produces a force of around 1200g – that's 1,200 times the force that gravity exerts on our bodies when we're just standing normally on the ground. Just to put that in perspective, we experience around 3.5g on a typical rollercoaster and we tend to suffer concussion at roughly 100g. So how does it manage this? It does it through four specialised parts of its head: its super-strong but elastic beak; its really long, curved hyoid bone, which curls from under its beak around the top of its head and under its eye to evenly distribute the force of drilling, kind of like an airbag; a large mass of spongy bone, which sits between its beak and its brain to stop the vibrations from reaching its brain; and the way the skull and the fluid that surrounds its brain interact with each other. It's the perfect shock absorber. And then there are the barbs on a woodpecker's tongue which help to spear the insects it's trying to catch. And the way it can listen to insects moving as it's tapping into wood.

GREEN WOODPECKER

Scientific name: *Picus viridis*

Conservation status (UK/Europe): Green/Least Concern

In three words: Large, loud, laugher!

Look out for: Olive-green back and wings, red cap, yellow bum

How easy it is to see them: Challenging – they blend into the background. Listen for the laugh, then look near grassy areas near trees where they'll be searching for ants

Also known as a Green Chicken, for reasons known only to my Mama, I love Green Woodpeckers. It always feels a bit special when you see one, because they're shy, they don't come to birdfeeders and you don't see them as much as the more common Great Spotted Woodpecker. You'll hear them quite a bit, though, because they make the most incredible call, known as yaffling, that sounds like hysterical laughter. You usually see them on the ground pecking at ants or rooting around a dead log. When they find a good anthill, they really go for it, and as they dig more, the ants get more and more annoyed and start climbing up the woodpecker, who's then shaking them off. You might well see one in a local park if you wait for long enough, especially if the grass has just been cut. They're about the size of a pigeon, have a really distinctive red head, olive-green backs and a black face between the eye and the long, strong bill. You can tell a male because it has a red stripe leading diagonally downwards from the base of the bill under its eye.

Green Woodpeckers are the largest of the three species of woodpecker that we get in the UK. Europe's a bit luckier on the woodpecker front. There's one species that is so annoyingly close to the UK that you could probably see from the White Cliffs of Dover with an enormous zoom lens. It's the Black Woodpecker, which is one of the largest woodpecker species in the world. It's nearly double the size of the Great Spotted, so we're talking about the same size as a Crow. Except you're unlikely to confuse it with a crow, not least because it has a bright red crown and distinctive white eye. It's common in forests (and urban parkland) across north and eastern Europe and the Balkans. There is the occasional rumoured sighting in the UK, but to my knowledge, nothing has ever been confirmed. Having said that, their numbers are increasing in northern France, and Woodpecker expert Gerard Gorman suggests it's only a matter of time before they make it over here. I'll be rolling out the red carpet!

Then there's the Middle Spotted Woodpecker, which does look similar to the Great Spotted but it has a red crown instead of a black one, a pink lower belly and a much paler face. It also doesn't have the black 'moustache' running from its beak. There's also the Three-toed Woodpecker, which is common in northern Europe, parts of central Europe, Russia and even Japan. It's just a bit smaller than the Great Spotted Woodpecker and is similarly black and white, although its flanks are white with black bars. Also, unlike the three woodpeckers we see in the UK, this one doesn't have any red colouring on its head, but the male does have a yellow crown. As you might expect, it only has three toes (it's missing the backwards-facing toe) that the three UK woodpeckers have. If you happen to be on holiday in Norway, Sweden or Finland, look for dead conifer trees, as this is where these guys make their nests.

NIGHTINGALE

Scientific name: *Luscinia megarhynchos*

Conservation status (UK/Europe): Red/Secure

In three words: Secretive, night-time soloist

Listen/look out for: Melodic, meaningful song with pauses in the middle and a final flourish; look for a brown, Robin-like bird skulking low down in cover

How easy it is to see them: Hard/Really Hard – follow the song in late spring, be really patient and good luck to you!

Not many people will have actually seen a Nightingale. That's partly because they're summer visitors to the UK and their range and numbers have been sadly diminishing. But it's also because these guys really don't want to be seen! They're classic lurkers, loitering in a bush or other dense vegetation. And on top of that, they're surprisingly plain-looking, mostly brown and grey birds, although they have got a slightly more colourful reddish-brown tail, which is often raised up. Catching sight of this legendary songster, who is slightly bigger than a Robin, can take patience, so when you do finally see it, I'm not sure I care that much about what it looks like, because seeing one is a reward in itself!

They're called Nightingales because they're famous for singing at night. But, other birds do this too, like Robins and Blackbirds, especially in towns and cities, so if you do hear one singing at night and you're in an urban setting, it's very unlikely to be a Nightingale. Sorry! They're very particular about the habitat they like. They prefer dense thickets, scrub and coppiced woodland (coppicing meaning cutting back trees to take away some of the canopy, which helps more light and heat reach the floor and allows woodland flowers and shrubs to establish themselves, and it's this sort of habitat the Nightingale really likes), often close to freshwater. A really interesting study carried out by Chas Holt of the British Trust for Ornithology (BTO) in

2010 in a wood in Suffolk showed that Nightingales really don't like areas that deer have been grazing in because they strip away the low vegetation that is such an important part of the bird's habitat. When I've been out listening for Nightingales, I've found that the best areas are the scrubby edges of woodland, where shrubs have just been allowed to roam free so they provide lots of cover, while giving them the woods they need to feed in. That's one of the reasons Berlin has had such success with the Tiergarten, their well-known 210-acre urban park. It hasn't been overly managed so there are lots of wild spaces and Germans have been encouraged to record Nightingale song on an app. The app can determine if the bird is actually a Nightingale, and if it is, it charts the location the song was heard in and shows it on an interactive map. From this data, you can get an idea of the locations Nightingales like to breed in. There are thought to be around 1,500 Nightingale pairs in Berlin, now, which is incredible! It shows what a bit of wild space can do, though. It's exactly why I encourage people to leave part of their lawns unmowed. Don't worry about what your neighbour might be thinking! If everything is neat and formal, like a planted forest, amazing birds like Nightingales haven't got any cover or protection because they'll be sheltering from the elements in shrubs. Letting nature do its thing is really helping there.

Bear in mind that Nightingales are only here from late April to early August (at best) and they'll only sing from the time they arrive here in late April to early June, so you need to be in the right place at the right time to hear them. But wow, is it worth it! They don't just sing at night, though – they will sing in the day too, and especially around dawn and dusk.

Trying to describe their song is difficult because it's just mesmerising, ranging from fast to slow, high-pitched to low-pitched with clear high notes, mournful whines, fast staccato sections, little chattery parts, all effortlessly blending into each other. It's endlessly variable and complicated, involving over 250 different 'phrases'. It's no wonder that their song has inspired poems, operas, fairy tales, folk tales, music, ballet, the list goes on. Also, when Nightingales start singing, you know that spring has really arrived. And once the song has been pointed out to you, you won't believe that it's coming from just one bird!

They breed throughout western, southern and central Europe, down into Turkey, parts of the Middle East and as far east as Mongolia. The UK is the northern limit of its range, and they can be found mostly in southern and eastern England, also Dorset and the Cotswolds. After the breeding season, they fly south to a wide strip of sub-Saharan Africa extending from Senegal to Ethiopia. That means a yearly total journey of around 7,000 miles – not bad for a bird that weighs the same as a small bag of crisps.

NUTHATCH

Scientific name: *Sitta europaea*

Conservation status (UK/Europe): Green/Secure

In three words: Climbs downwards headfirst

Look out for: Blue back, Zorro-like black mask; nesting hole surrounded by mud

How easy it is to see them: Challenging – but they will visit garden feeders and you'll see them if you wait for long enough in woodland!

With their dark eyestripe, these guys always remind me of Zorro. But if you can't see its face, the first thing to look out for is a bird moving down a tree headfirst, because a Nuthatch is the only bird in the UK that can do this. So, if you think what you're looking at is a Nuthatch, check and see which way it's moving on a tree. If it's moving downwards, it's a Nuthatch; if it's moving upwards, it's a Treecreeper.

Nuthatches can also hang upside down from branches. It's pretty impressive, and they can do it because of their specialised backward-facing toe called the hallux. It's long, curves down and looks like a claw. They'll often start at the top of one tree, move down it looking for insects and larvae and then carry on at the top of the next tree. Unlike creepers and woodpeckers, their strong feet mean they don't need to use their tail as a kind of prop, which is why a Nuthatch's tail is short.

They will turn up at garden feeders as well, for a bit of free grub, especially near trees and after a cold snap when they're looking for an energy hit, and they do forage on the ground for fallen berries and nuts. They use nest boxes, but often jazz them up by plastering mud around the entrance to make the opening just the right size! They do this by mixing mud with their saliva, which works really well as a bonding agent. So if you see a nest box that looks like someone's lobbed a load of mud at it, there's a very good chance there's a Nuthatch family inside.

The bad news for me, anyway, is that you don't see Nuthatches in the Highlands. They don't seem to like it any further north than Edinburgh. Shame – they're missing out! You will see Nuthatches in woods and gardens in England and Wales, though, and it's exciting when you do, because they're a slightly more unusual bird compared to the House Sparrow, Starling, Robins, Blue Tits and Blackbirds that you'll probably see in your garden quite a bit.

So, why's it called a Nuthatch then? Because of its habit of using a crevice to hold a nut, while it breaks it open with its beak.

SPARROWHAWK

Scientific name: *Accipiter nisus*

Conservation status (UK/Europe): Amber/Secure

In three words: Stealthy, low-flying hunter

Look out for: Other birds suddenly scattering; its long yellow legs; piercing yellow eyes, horizontally barred chest

How easy it is to see them: Challenging – look for them perched on fences, sitting on tree stumps plucking prey and in branches wherever you find songbirds; piles of plucked feathers can be a giveaway

Sparrowhawks breed in woods but you can find them all over the place, from cities to open countryside. They're the bird of prey you're most likely to see in your garden, because, as you've probably guessed already, they hunt small birds like Sparrows, Starlings and Tits, but female Sparrowhawks, which are much larger, can take down something as large as a Woodpigeon. Even so, Sparrowhawks are quite small as birds of prey go – not that much larger than a Jay.

Their short, rounded wings and long tail give them amazing aerial agility, allowing them to find their way through trees, squeeze through tiny gaps and bank around obstacles to zero in on their prey. They keep really low to the ground, skimming over fences, small plants and hedges and then rise up to surprise their victim. They're smart birds, learning to follow the same aerial pathway to a good source of prey, like a garden feeder. With a couple of powerful wingbeats, they reach attack speed and then use a combination of glides and wing beats to approach their target.

Your best chance of knowing that a Sparrowhawk is nearby is from a sudden change in the behaviour of songbirds in your garden. If lots of songbirds all start frantically calling or if Pigeons and Starlings suddenly flush (fly away suddenly and hurriedly), and you're not sure what's caused it, it can be a telltale sign there's a Sparrowhawk on the hunt. Otherwise, you might well see one perched in a tree, on a fence or on a roof overlooking a garden. At first glance, you might mistake one for a Peregrine Falcon or maybe even a Kestrel, but their eyes are the first giveaway. They have striking yellow irises (becoming orange when they get older), whereas Peregrines' and Kestrels' eyes are completely dark. Also, Sparrowhawks have long, thin legs and talons, helping them spring from the tree or roof they're waiting on like an Olympic swimmer diving from a starting block. These legs also help them pick up their prey, sometimes with just one talon, while they're swooping over it. Sparrowhawks do look similar to Goshawks, but Goshawks are much rarer, bigger (more like the size of a Buzzard) and you won't see them in gardens. Plus, adult Goshawks have a distinctive white eyestripe above the eye. Another bird that they look similar to is the Cuckoo, and that's a bit of evolutionary trickery that allows the Cuckoo to fool its victim into thinking it's a hunting Sparrowhawk. The victim flees, which lets the Cuckoo lay its egg in the nest of its victim, so the female can raise the chick as its own, which pushes the other eggs out of the nest. Clever and fiendish!

Female Sparrowhawks are up to 25 per cent larger than males, with some of them weighing up to twice the male. Females are also a slightly different colour, with their brownish-grey backs and brown barring on their underparts. Males are more colourful, with bluish-grey on top and reddish-brown barred breasts. Both have a relatively small bill, which they use to tear their prey apart from a plucking post – a favourite spot, like a tree stump.

Sparrowhawks have earned a reputation for being responsible for the decrease in the number of songbirds, but it's not true. The number of Sparrowhawks is limited by the amount of food around and the available nesting sites. If the number of songbirds goes up, so does the number of Sparrowhawks. And if the number of songbirds goes down, so does the number of Sparrowhawks. They're innocent! And having a Sparrowhawk visit your garden isn't just a wonderful sight, it's also a good sign that lots of songbirds are around, which means there's a healthy ecosystem right there outside your window.

These guys are like the jet fighters of close combat woodland. You'll never really see them in open moorland and, if you do, they're probably just moving through. What they rely on is the element of surprise and they're built to dodge and weave, even dislocating their shoulders backwards in flight to get through tiny gaps and come back out the other side at full speed. Their tail is like a massive rudder that allows for quick slow-down and change in direction. Sparrowhawks are happy to pluck a bird in front of you. I've had Sparrowhawks look at me dead in the eye on a lawn while I'm doing the washing up, making sure I'm not moving any closer. Or if you see a big pile of feathers on a lawn, it might well be a Sparrowhawk. A garden feeder is a bit like a McDonald's Drive Thru for a Sparrowhawk, and they'll suddenly appear over a hedge and snatch a bird, taking it off with them if it's small enough, or eating it right there if it's a larger bird.

TAWNY OWL

Scientific name: *Stryx aluco*

Conservation status (UK/Europe): Amber/Secure

In three words: Camouflaged, vocal, territorial

Look out for them in: Holes and crevices in trees or among ivy wrapped around a tree trunk; occasionally perched on a fence

How easy it is to see them: Challenging – sometimes even when you're looking straight at them!

There's so much to say about these incredible birds, I'm not even sure where to start! OK, here goes...

It always surprises people how small these guys actually are. They only weigh about as much as a Carrion Crow or a Wood Pigeon, usually around 500g, although females are a lot bigger than males, like almost all birds of prey. It isn't fully understood why female birds of prey are bigger than males; the reverse is true among the vast majority of birds. It might well be something to do with the female needing to be able to defend the nest against predators. Because she'll be incubating eggs and rearing chicks while the male's out foraging, she needs her size to be able to look after her own!

OK – here's a really good fact that even people who don't have the remotest interest in birds *do* find fascinating: the 'ter-witt-too-wooooo' sound that everyone associates with owls? No single owl actually makes that sound. But they do between a male and female pair of Tawny Owls! That's right, it's a duet! She goes 'kee-wick' (which does sound a bit like 'ter-witt') and he goes 'hoo-hoo-hoo-hoo'. I always used to get this wrong, though, because someone once told me: 'The Twit is the male', which makes sense because it does sound like she's calling him a twit! To be fair, the duet goes more like: he goes 'hoo-hoo-hoo-hooooo' and she might answer with her 'ker-wick' call. It is actually pretty easy to imitate the call of the male by cupping your hands and blowing into the hole between them. A study that appeared in the British Trust for Ornithology's journal, *Bird Study*, in 1994 showed that in 94 per cent of known territories, you'd receive an answering call within half an hour. And I can believe that, because Tawnies are so territorial they will get back to you sharpish!

You'll hear these calls at night although males do occasionally hoot during the day, especially in autumn when young birds are trying to tell everyone this is their territory, even their parents! Tawny Owls are nocturnal creatures but they do sometimes hunt in the daytime if they've got hungry mouths to feed. If you're lucky, you might see one roosting in the day in a tree or even on a fence post. They are very well camouflaged though, with their brown-grey feathers to blend into the trunks and branches of trees, so you'll need to look carefully. At first glance, they really do just look like bits of wood!

Tawnies are common across the UK and almost all of Europe, except northern parts of Scandinavia. One place they aren't native to, though, is Ireland. And so, when one was heard (and then spotted) in 2013 in County Down, Northern Ireland, it caused huge excitement among birders. It had probably veered off course during the recent storms there. Let's hope it found a mate and has started something special on the Emerald Isle.

So how do they hunt at night? Well, they have all sorts of adaptations that make them really good at it.

Their short, broad wings and short tail enable them to manoeuvre through trees, glide and hover over prey. The wing's leading edges (the front of the wing as the bird's in flight) are shaped like a big comb, with fine serrations, and these break up turbulent air (the air that makes that woooshing sound). And then there are the soft, furry edges on the trailing edge of the wing which help absorb the sound the wings make. The result is pretty much silent flight, so that its prey can't hear it, but also so that the owl can track its prey without being distracted by the sound of its own wings.

Their eyesight is about twice as sensitive as ours in dim light, but they can't see in complete darkness. Now here's a weird fact: owls can't actually move their eyes. That's because they don't have eyeballs. They're more like tubes or cylinders that are held in place by specialised structures in the skull. Owls compensate for not being able to move their eyes with their unbelievably flexible necks. We're talking twice as many vertebrae as humans have. And this helps owls to turn their heads not in a full circle, as you might have been told (!) but up to 270°, which is still incredible.

Also, their ears aren't evenly positioned, either horizontally or vertically! An owl's left ear (the right one if you're looking at the owl) is actually slightly lower than the right one. This means that sounds reach the ears at slightly different times, and it's this that helps an owl to pinpoint where the sound has come from in the pitch black. It's exactly how triangulation works with the GPS on your phone, with signals bouncing off two satellites at slightly different times to pinpoint your location!

A Tawny Owl also has a great spatial memory, and that's really handy when you barely ever leave your territory, so you end up getting to know it extremely well. And that's so important when food is scarce. Tawnies are well known for putting up an amazingly fierce defence of their nest. To the point that bird ringers trying to monitor and ring young Tawnies sometimes have to go into battle wearing crash helmets! I remember being in Roman Camp – a hilltop wildlife haven near Bangor, in North Wales, and I got a call from a friend saying that a Tawny Owl chick had just fallen out of the nest. I tend to get calls like this! But I had a feeling it was a fledgling that was out of the nest for a reason, so I said, 'Just leave it – I bet you it starts climbing back up the tree.' When I got there, I spotted the mother, just a couple of trees away watching everything we were doing. As one of us got a little too close to her, we could hear the warning beak 'claps' and we knew to back off! One of my friends wasn't so lucky, though, coming back slightly worse for wear from the pub. The Tawny Owl was giving him the warning beak claps, but he didn't notice, and then, whack!

Tawnies are seriously well camouflaged. I remember being out with a good birder friend of mine called Robin, and he sent me a message saying 'Tawny Owl up at the tree ahead'. And I looked at the tree and couldn't see anything. So I sent him a message asking where he'd seen it. 'It's in the little nook' came the reply. So I scanned the tree again, for about ten minutes in the end, even walking round the whole thing, but for the life of me, I couldn't see a nook! It was only when it half opened its eyes that I realised I'd been staring at it the whole time. It had just had its eyes closed, and it was sitting in the hole of the tree Robin was talking about. And with its eyes closed and only some of its head visible, its pattern is so well camouflaged it's completely invisible! Bear in mind that ivy is one of their favourite places to hide in.

Tawnies are one of the earliest-nesting birds of prey in the UK, usually laying their first eggs in mid-March. Some are already on eggs in February. They're tough birds, and I've seen this first hand. Sometimes they do get clipped by lorries and cars, and I've seen them sitting at the side of the road looking completely dazed, but after a bit of rehabilitation, they can make a full recovery.

WRYNECK

Scientific name: *Jynx torquilla*

Conservation status (UK/Europe): Former breeder/ Depleted

In three words: Amazing neck dancer

Look out for: Starling-sized bird with a pointy head and beak looking for ants on the ground

How easy it is to see them: Hard – but look out for them in August and September along the east and south coasts of the UK

The Wryneck is a bit like the Holy Grail for birders because you just wouldn't believe some of the things it can do!

First of all, a Wryneck is a rare and unusual member of the woodpecker family. A hundred years ago, it was a pretty common breeding bird in the UK, but by the 1970s it had become a rare migrant along the southern and eastern coasts of England, Orkney and Shetland on their way south. Wrynecks spend their winters in Africa, below the Sahara in a strip that runs all the way from Senegal on the west coast to Ethiopia in the east. You can occasionally see them in spring as well on their way back from Africa to breeding grounds in Europe. It's a really small woodpecker (we're talking only a bit bigger than a sparrow). And its colour – wow, it's like a forest floor in autumn with its mottled browns, greys and buff colouring, which is handy because that's where it spends most of its time, hoovering up ants with its surprisingly long tongue. Don't expect to see these guys climbing up trunks or branches – they're not like other woodpeckers. And its beak is a bit unusual too, smaller and sharper than other woodpeckers', and that's because it doesn't need to drill into wood. It nests in holes that are already there.

So, why is it called a Wryneck? Well, that's because it can do something absolutely amazing, and that's bend its head all the way back and twist it in every direction you can imagine, almost like a cobra rearing its head up. And that's no accident – it's thought to mimic a snake – it even hisses too! – when it feels threatened, and predators can panic and let it go. You have to see it to really believe it.

As for its name, 'Wry' was a verb used from the 16th century to mean 'twist or turn'. And its Latin name might be my favourite in this book – *Jynx torquilla*. *Torquilla* comes from the Medieval Latin word *torquere*, which also means 'twist' but 'Jynx' comes from the Greek word *iunx*. And it turns out Iunx was a nymph who enchanted the god Zeus to fall in love with Io, the princess of Argos. Zeus's wife wasn't very happy about this, as you can imagine, and turned her into a bird – the Wryneck (which became known as 'jynx'). Wrynecks were considered so curious that they were used in witchcraft and divination, and so sometime in the 17th century, 'jynx' came to mean 'charm' or 'spell'. I've heard a lot of old birders just call Wrynecks 'Jynx' as a nickname.

When you're on holiday, look out for Wrynecks in open ground near the southern and eastern coasts of England in August, September and October – especially near anthills. They've got maybe a dozen fine dark bars along their sandy-coloured throats, with the bars becoming like little T-shapes along their breasts. They've also got a brown stripe running from their brown eyes to the back of their heads and another one running down their backs.

MOORS AND MOUNTAINS

This is a section dear to my heart because I'm lucky enough to have both moors and mountains behind my house on the west coast of Scotland. And I'm luckier still because there are Golden Eagles up in those mountains! I've spent a lot of time watching a local pair of them near me from hides that I've built myself, with a bit of help from local friends and fellow camera folk. It's a lovely community and everyone pitches in to help each other out on their home projects, hobbies and livelihood (in my case!).

The open spaces that you find on moorland are perfect for unusual birds of prey that you might not have heard of, like the incredible Merlin – the smallest European Falcon – who will chase small birds at high speed very close to the ground, and the ghostlike Hen Harrier zigzagging silently across open ground looking for rodents. Moorland is also used as the display site for incredible birds like the Black Grouse to try and win a mate. It's quite a spectacle with females gathering around the edge of the arena while the males show off.

I get really excited if I see any of the birds in this section, like the famously approachable Dotterel, which you might even stumble across on a plateau if you're hiking in the Cairngorms in Scotland or a European mountain range. And the Dotterel is a bird that not a lot of people have heard of, but I want to change that because it's really unusual and pretty extraordinary. And then there's the stunning Dartford Warbler that I'm fairly sure knows how pretty it is because it likes to make itself as visible as possible at the top of gorse and other shrubs dotted among moorland. But I'm so pleased that it does, because that is one sexy bird.

BLACK GROUSE

Scientific name: *Tetrao tetrix*

Conservation status (UK/Europe): Red/Least Concern

In three words: Confident, loud performer

Look/listen out for: Red flap above eye (male), black plumage and tail (white underneath) that curls around at edges; display sites are often areas of shortish grass among denser vegetation in moorland – listen out for bubbling and hissing sounds from males; mottled grey-brown females assemble at edge of arena

How easy it is to see them: Fairly Easy – if you head to their habitat, you've got a pretty good chance of seeing them

The first time I saw a Black Grouse, I was asleep in my car (not all my anecdotes start like this) on the top of a hill in a place called World's End in Denbighshire, North Wales, and I got woken up by a bird calling at 4 o'clock in the morning. I wound down the window, but it was still dark and I couldn't see anything until the sun came up. Then, eventually, I was rewarded, as I was well placed to watch them strut their stuff at the *lek* I'd been told about (which is basically a specific area of open ground that male animals come together in to perform courtship displays. *Lek* is a Swedish word, which means 'play'). The males fan their tails, puff themselves up, droop their wings down, chase each other about and make all sorts of bubbling and gurgling noises. It's quite a performance!

You're most likely to see them on the ground, but if you do surprise one, they'll flap away quickly and you'll see the white wingstripe along the top of its wings. The only bird that you might visually confuse with a Black Grouse is a Capercaillie, but it's unlikely because they prefer different habitats (Black Grouse are also significantly smaller – think hen-sized). Black Grouses like moorland and farmland, particularly areas near trees. They've both got a red 'wattle' above their eyes but the one on the Capercaillie is a small semicircle – the Black Grouse's wattle is more like a big, bright red stick-on eyebrow.

There are a few thousand in Scotland – the Cairngorms National Park and Loch Lomond and the

Trossachs National Parks are good spots to find them, but in England and Wales, you can only really see them in central North Wales and the North Pennines. Sadly, after 1998, they could no longer be found in the Peak District. They used to be common in southern and central England but habitat loss and overgrazing has hit them hard and they're still on the Red List in the UK, although it's happier news in Europe, where they're doing fine.

There have been a few conservation efforts, including the partnership between The Famous Grouse (the whisky guys) and the RSPB. This started in 2008 after the company launched its Black Grouse whisky and donated 50p of every sale for the first three years after its launch. That has helped improve the habitat across seven different RSPB reserves (five in Scotland, one in North Wales and one in England) and lek numbers do seem to be increasing, which is amazing news.

CAPERCAILLIE

Scientific name: *Tetrao urogallus*
Conservation status (UK/Europe): Red/Depleted
In three words: Loud, aggressive, rare
Look out for: (male): A huge, Turkey-sized black grouse with red crescent over eye and an incredible fan-like upright tail during display; females are much smaller, are mottled-grey with red breast patch and watch the males from trees above display area; Capercaillies roost in treetops so look out for a large shape in pine trees
How easy it is to see them: Hard – bear in mind that all the places to see them are under protection, so it's advised not to travel to them unless with a guide; Capercaillie population in Scandinavia is much larger

These guys are the largest members of the grouse family in Scotland and they are truly magnificent birds. Capercaillie comes from a Gaelic word that means 'horse of the forest'. And that's fair, because males can weigh up to 5kg, which is about the same as a Turkey. They're dark grey, with iridescent green and blue on their heads, necks and breasts and with a ring of red skin around their eyes. They're nearly twice the size of females, who are brownish with silver and black barring and a rusty breast patch. Capercaillies are only found in small areas of native pinewoods and commercial conifer plantations in four areas of northern Scotland.

I know one of the few places in the UK you can walk from to see a *lek*. The first I heard of this *lek* site was when I was on a country estate filming Golden Eagles that had taken up residence there, and one of the people running the estate said: 'Did you see the Capercaillies on the way? And I said: 'Wait, what?!' I ended up taking a whole day off to head up there, just before dawn, and then this male appears out of nowhere, strutting his stuff. It was the best thing ever. They are certainly full of themselves and aren't afraid of anything, however big you are, and will properly try and chase you off!

They are really vulnerable to habitat disturbance and their numbers in the UK have declined from around 20,000 in the 1970s. A survey carried out by RSPB Scotland in 2022 estimated that only 542 Capercaillies were left in Scotland. That's a 50 per cent decrease in numbers since the last survey six years before. They're in real danger of becoming extinct, but this would actually be for the second time. Capercaillies became extinct in the UK in the 18th century, and there were various attempts to reintroduce them in the early part of the 19th century, but none of them succeeded in establishing a 'wild' population. And then, in 1837, fifty-five young birds from Sweden were reintroduced to Taymouth Castle, in Perthshire, and the local pinewoods proved to be the perfect habitat for them. They were also protected to some extent from predators. It's actually the only successful reintroduction of a member of the grouse family in history.

DARTFORD WARBLER

Scientific name: *Sylvia undata*
Conservation status (UK/Europe): Amber/Near Threatened
In three words: Visible, stunning, cheeky
Look out for: Singing from the top of a gorse stem; darting in and out of bushes; red eye ring
How easy it is to see them: Challenging – try heathland in south and west of England, France, Spain, Portugal and Italy

This is a sexy bird and they're making a comeback, after nearly becoming extinct in the UK after the really cold winter of 1962/3 left only ten surviving pairs. Dartford Warblers only eat insects and spiders, so when snow is covering the ground, it struggles to find anything to sustain it.

The Dartford Warbler has a beautiful red eye ring, reddish brown underparts, grey-brown upperparts and a long, dark grey tail. You might recognise it, however, from its scratchy, rattling quick warble that it sings from a top of a gorse stem. I don't know if it's just me, but whenever I see one on a lovely coconut-smelling gorse bush (they'll sit there happily enough), and I try and raise my camera even an inch, they'll be long gone! So there might have been a few occasions where I've waved my fist in the direction of a teasing Dartford Warbler, muttering, 'You little...!' They are such beautiful birds though and I could watch them for hours. It's not just the amazing colour, it's their shape and stance as well, with their tail slightly cocked like a Wren.

They like heathland with low scrubby heather and gorse, but in the UK their range is still fairly limited to Surrey, Hampshire (the New Forest is a good place to find them), Dorset, Exmoor, Suffolk and South Wales. There are some good UK holiday destinations in there, so watch out for it if you're in any of those places in late spring. Don't expect to see them in Dartford, though – they were only called that by the Welsh naturalist Thomas Pennant who was given a couple of specimens near Bexleyheath, which is only a few miles away from Dartford in Kent.

You can also find them in Spain, western France, southern Italy and north Africa, although their range is shifting northwards mainly as a consequence of climate change, and their numbers in those places are declining rapidly. Part of the reason their numbers have recovered well in the UK is because winters have been milder here. This means that the UK is likely to host more and more Dartford Warblers. The other reason their numbers have increased here is that some heathland is being better protected and managed. Dartford Warblers nest on or very close to the ground, in heather and gorse, and sometimes near to paths, which makes them really vulnerable to disturbance. A nearby dog can make parent birds leave the nest, meaning their eggs and chicks are at risk from predators, so everyone will thank you if you stick to the paths!

DOTTEREL

Scientific name: *Charadrius morinellus*

Conservation status (UK/Europe): Red/Least Concern

In three words: Approachable, unexpectedly colourful

Look out for: A little group of what look like small, moving rocks in the Highlands or mountainous terrain in Scandinavia

How easy it is to see them: Hard – most commonly seen in Scotland's mountains and Norway, but can be seen near the coast of eastern England during spring and autumn migration

Most people have never heard of a Dotterel, so welcome to those in the know! It's made it into the exclusive list of birds I've covered in this book partly because they're fond of high places, like the Highlands, and the Highlands are dear to my heart. But anytime I've gone out on a mission to find a Dotterel nest, I've never succeeded! I've only seen Dotterels a handful of times in my life, and it's been a happy accident, on a walk up in the Cairngorms or the west coast where the snowy mountain caps meet the moorland. And each time, I've thought, *that looks like a rock that's just moved in front of me – oh no, wait, it's a Dotterel.* They're so confident with their camouflage that they know you're not going to see them. And they'll only move off literally when you practically step on them.

The Dotterel is a member of the Plover family (which also includes Lapwings). You might have heard of a Ringed Plover – they're cute little wading birds with brown caps, white foreheads and a black band that looks a bit like a neckerchief. If you're on your holidays, you'll probably see a Ringed Plover on a beach or in a harbour. But unlike most Plovers, Dotterels like high mountaintops. They're about the same length as a Starling, but plumper. That's only a useful comparison when they're on the ground, though. In flight, the Dotterel's wings are much longer and swept back.

Dotterels are on the Red List of UK birds, which means, unless things change, their future is looking a bit uncertain. Thankfully, it's a better story in northern Scandinavia and northern Russia, where their breeding numbers are higher and more stable. A lot of people come up to the Highlands to see Golden Eagles, and I can't blame them – those incredible birds are part of the reason I moved up to Scotland – but there are even fewer Dotterels in the UK than there are Golden Eagles. There are only a few hundred, and they only come here for the summer, arriving in April and leaving by August. Dotterels come dressed for the occasion wearing their Sunday best, which they change out of after they head back to northern Africa for the winter. From the back, they're perfectly camouflaged with their grey-brown neck and wings, but if you catch sight of their undersides, you're in for a surprise. With their chestnut-coloured bellies bordered by a V-shaped black-and-white ribbon that almost looks like it's holding an invisible medal in the middle of it, they're seriously pretty birds. They've also got a crescent-moon-shaped white eyestripe and a jet-black area on the belly. So it's like they're wearing two outfits – one practical and sensible so they blend into the background, and one for party time! Plus, if you do see one, you'll be richly rewarded because these guys are famously trusting and approachable, so you'll get a really good look.

It's a woman's world for a Dotterel – unlike almost every other UK and European bird, the females are more brightly coloured than the males. And that gives a clue that everything's a bit different for Dotterels. It's the female that does the courting and displaying, competing for access to the males, and they'll mate with several males, while the male only mates with one female (known as polyandry). The male is the one who incubates the eggs for 21–9 days. Meanwhile, the female has another clutch of eggs between four and 11 days later. The males provide all the parental care to the chicks. Polyandry is really rare in birds – it only happens in less than 1 per cent of all bird species and mostly in waders (known in the US as 'shorebirds').

And then there's the name 'Dotterel' which is a bit unusual, too. In Gaelic, it's known as Amadan Mointeach, which amazingly translates as 'Mossfool' or 'The Foolish Fellow of the Peat Mosses'. In English, Dotterel comes from 'dote' which means 'foolish' or 'senile' – you might have heard someone insultingly called a 'dotard' in *Game of Thrones* or another medieval drama. It's all a bit harsh because the Dotterel is only called that because it's friendly and easy to catch! It's not known whether the insult or the bird's name came first, but the name dates back to 1440. Its association with being tame even extends to its scientific name *Charadrius morinellus*, with the latter word coming from the Greek word *moros* for, you've guessed it: 'foolish'. Time for renaming, I'd say. We can't be punishing folks for being friendly, now can we?

GOLDEN EAGLE

Scientific name: *Aquila chrysaetos*

Conservation status (UK/Europe): Green/Secure

In four words: Massive, powerful, determined, secretive

Look out for: A dot in the distance soaring over mountains in Scotland and Europe, especially Norway, Italy, Spain, Switzerland

How easy it is to see them: Hard – you'll need binoculars and to be in the right place

There's something magical about Golden Eagles. The name helps a bit, because it sets these incredible birds apart, like they're the Kings of Birds. And to be honest, I buy into that, because there is something regal about them. They're strong, fearless, like to live in remote, clifftop castles (or very tall trees), people travel great distances to get a glimpse of them and they have much finer tastes when it comes to food.

I imagine some of you have seen a picture of a Golden Eagle and you're thinking 'It's brown?!', and you're right, it is, except for a small area of golden-brown feathers on the back of their heads and necks. They are huge birds, second only to the White-tailed Eagle in terms of wingspan and weight in the UK, but we're still talking 200–220cm worth of wing and up to 6.6kg in weight (females are larger than males, who are rarely above 4.5kg). Their wings are wide and rounded, which helps them soar effortlessly and you'll probably see one in the distance, slowly circling a high peak. You might be able to make out their 'fingered' feathers, so called because they look like a series of separated digits.

People do confuse Buzzards with Golden Eagles, and to be fair, their colours and shape aren't a million miles away. But the places you find them *are* a million miles away. You'll see Buzzards a lot in the countryside all over the UK, fearlessly lurking on fence posts near roads looking for carrion. With a couple of local exceptions (which I'll get to), you'll only find Golden Eagles over high peaks in the Highlands of Scotland and will need a Zoom lens to see them, unless you've managed to build a hide next to their eyrie (the name for an eagle's nest)! Size can be difficult to gauge when they're flying, but Golden Eagles really are huge, at least three times the weight of a Buzzard. That's not to say Buzzards aren't impressive, though. It's pretty amazing seeing a bird of prey that close to you when you're on the motorway! If you do manage to get close to a Golden Eagle, you feel how much power they have. They ooze it, and it never ceases to amaze me even when I've been sitting in a hide for 15 hours and it's –4 degrees. Being just maybe 8 or 9 metres away from such an incredible bird with my long lens, zooming in so I can see the colour of its eyes, is incredible.

When I was filming the Golden Eagle pair (who I've nicknamed Lady and the Assassin) not far from my house, I spent three weeks in a hide, twelve hours a day. A grand total of 252 hours. I slept in my car, although I'm no stranger to that! I took over 2,500 photographs and kept 25 of them. To be honest, I only really like three of them, but it was still worth the three weeks I spent getting them. I've been in hides for longer periods, too, sometimes spending 24/7 there doing your whole business there.

Inside, I'm hunched over and I've got just enough space to fold my arms or put an extra jacket on, but that's it. Luckily, I seem to be quite good at coping with the cold, and you need to be when it's below freezing and you're wiggling your toes to stay warm, but it's so cold that you can't actually tell if they're wiggling or not! If you move or twitch when you're looking at eagles, with their eyesight, they'll know something isn't right immediately, and then they might not return for another month! So you have to be super-aware of yourself. Your hearing becomes so finely attuned to everything that's happening around you. The things that you usually do unconsciously, like scratch, shift your weight, tilt etc., you have to be in control of. There's definitely no munching on crisps or opening fizzy drinks, so you learn to eat soft fruit like oranges and bananas and drink diluted juice. The amount of noise you're making does make a big difference depending on which animal you're dealing with though. With Golden Eagles, you have to be absolutely still and silent. If it's just chicks, they don't care at all. You can have a disco and they won't mind!

I've spent a lot of time in that hide filming my local Golden Eagle pair. Lady is a big female, a graceful Lady of the sky, while the Assassin, the male, is a bruiser. He's a bit like a lightweight boxer: fast, dynamic, always on the move and always on a mission. He'll catch foxes and bring them back to the eyrie. That shows you how strong these guys are – an adult red fox is about 6kg. And that may not sound like a lot, but bear in mind that the Assassin is probably only 4–4.5kg. To take down an animal like a fox and bring it back to your nest is quite some feat, really.

I imagine a chat between Lady and the Assassin going something like this:

'Right, what would you like for dinner, my Lady? Fox, badger, rabbit or do you fancy something a bit more salty, like gannet or redshank?' Golden Eagles don't generally like to hunt over water – they want to be inland when they hunt most of the time, but Lady and the Assassin have chosen an eyrie on a clifftop facing the water, so they can go for surf or turf for dinner.

In 2018, Golden Eagles were reintroduced in the Scottish Borders and Dumfries and Galloway. This was a plan over ten years in the making, involving eaglets from the Highlands that have been moved south. The South of Scotland Golden Eagle Project are the guys behind it and it was all quite hush-hush to begin with, with five specially built aviaries built in secret locations in the Southern Uplands of Scotland. Five eaglets arrived in 2018 and stayed there for two months before they were released into the Moffat Hills. There are now thought to be nearly 40 of them in southern Scotland, which is amazing news. And on the amazing news front, Golden Eagles were also reintroduced to Ireland in 2001, in Glenveagh National Park near the north coast. The first wild Golden Eagle chick to hatch in Ireland in a hundred years happened in 2007. Like with The South of Scotland Golden Eagle

Project, eaglets were moved from the Highlands and the location was kept secret.

Although there are only about five hundred pairs of Golden Eagles in the UK, they're actually the most widely distributed eagle in the world, breeding in Scandinavia, southern Europe, Russia, Central Asia and northern Japan. So if you're in any of these places near mountains, keep your eyes peeled!

HEN HARRIER

Scientific name: *Circus cyaneus*
Conservation status (UK/Europe): Red/Near Threatened
In three words: Grey fluttering ghost
Look out for: A bird flying in a zigzag pattern no more than 3 metres off the ground over moorlands; white bum; blue-grey back and black wingtips (male); brown, barred tail (female)
How easy it is to see them: Challenging – easier in winter as range expands across open country

Whenever someone asks me to describe a Hen Harrier, I tell them to imagine mixing a Barn Owl with a hawk. They've got the framed, dish-shaped face of an owl, but with the eyes and beak of a hawk or a Buzzard. It's unique and beautiful. Males stand out more with their black wingtips and incredible pale blue-grey faces, back and wings, and that's what gives them the nickname 'ghosts'.

Females (and juveniles) are mostly brown, with yellowish-brown undersides and dark brown streaks. They both have a long, barred tail, which is why they've ended up with the nickname 'ringtail'. You can easily mistake a female or juvenile Hen Harrier for a Buzzard from a distance, but you can tell them apart from the way that they fly. Hen Harriers float like a butterfly and sting like a bee, to quote Muhammad Ali. Hen Harriers fly slowly, low down over open ground, a hunting technique called 'quartering', listening and looking for small mammals on the ground. Buzzards fly in a straight line, then they'll catch a thermal (a column of rising air), let that do the hard work and then they'll circle high up. Hen Harriers zigzag in and out of a field, like they're changing their minds and chatting to themselves, saying something like 'No, I don't like that one', 'I'm not sure about that corner', 'Let's go check over here'.

If you're still not sure, look for a bright white bum. And it's that feature that sets them apart from everything else, including the other two harriers that breed in the

UK (the Marsh Harrier and the Montagu's Harrier). The
Marsh Harrier has come back from the brink, because
in 1971, there was only one breeding pair in the UK, in
Minismere in Suffolk, making it the UK's rarest bird of
prey. Three things had come together to threaten its
survival: persecution, habitat loss, and the widespread
use of pesticides like DDT after the Second World War,
which can cause serious nervous system damage and thin
their eggshells, so some embryos wouldn't survive. Now,
thanks to insecticide bans, habitat restoration projects
and legal protection under the Wildlife and Countryside
Act of 1981, Marsh Harriers now number in the hundreds.
These guys are really fond of East Anglia, where they
mainly breed in reedbeds, but their range is expanding
and they're now found in marshlands in Somerset, Kent,
Lancashire, Yorkshire and parts of central and northern
Scotland. They have a large, but slightly patchy range
across Europe with the biggest populations in western
Russia, Finland and Spain.

Female and young Marsh Harriers can look like
Hen Harriers, so look out for the ringed tail in the Hen
Harrier and the pale head in the Marsh Harrier. Male
Marsh Harriers are more distinctive with their brown
and grey wings with black wingtips and reddy brown
belly. Montagu's Harriers are summer visitors and they're
sadly so rare (under ten breeding pairs) that you're very
unlikely to see one.

Hen Harriers get their names from the animals they used to prey on a long time ago, but they mainly hunt small mammals and small birds now. They do go for grouse chicks, especially during breeding season, which makes them very unpopular with gamekeepers. That's why their UK population is only around 550 breeding pairs, and almost all of these are in Scotland. But Hen Harriers do fly over from continental Europe for the winter, arriving in October and November, and are more widely distributed across England during that time. Hen Harriers like different habitats for hunting according to the season. In summer, they're often found over heather moors, but in winter they prefer marshy areas, farmland and heathland.

Hen Harriers keep their wings above the horizontal, so they form a V-shape in flight. They tend to like windy uplands so they can glide against the wind and keep up a low ground speed, which helps them find voles in dense, low cover and small birds. Then they drop suddenly and silently. They are amazing acrobats, and the males show this off big time during their display flights in springtime to try and attract a female. We're talking quick turns, somersaults and then plummeting towards the ground, spinning or twisting until he's just a few feet from the ground before rising again and repeating it. It's spectacular. And a bit mental to be honest. It's earned them the nickname 'skydancer' but even that doesn't quite do it justice!

MERLIN

Scientific name: *Falco columbarius*

Conservation status (UK/Europe): Red/Least Concern

In three words: Fidgety, flappy, fast

Look out for: Greyer than a Kestrel, but similar-looking; sat on a stump, grassy mound or a fence post

How easy it is to see them: Hard – they're so quick and small but it's easier in winter as range expands to lowland and coasts

I wanted to include one of the Kestrel, Hobby or Merlin in this book, but I'm going to end up talking about all of them here, so you've got three for the price of one! They're all Falcons, like the Peregrine, only smaller, and you'll find them in different places and different times doing different things, which makes them easier to tell apart. You'll have seen a Kestrel, because they hover over roadsides, holding their tails in a fan shape, occasionally swooping down for a closer look at a little rodent scurrying around below. This has given them the nickname 'Motorway Hawk', which is a little on the unfair side because you'll find them all over the place, from coasts to countryside. From underneath, they're barred and quite pale with a dark band to the end of their tail, but from the top, they're a rich, reddy brown colour with a blue-grey head. Hobbies and Merlins are probably our least well-known birds of prey, which I've always found a bit strange because they're beautiful and amazingly acrobatic. It's probably because they're small and harder to catch sight of. Unlike the Kestrel, you won't see them hovering. These guys are both built for speed.

The Hobby is a summer visitor from Africa and they don't tend to fly further north than Yorkshire. You might see one flash past, catching sight of its rusty red 'trousers' as it banks left and right on its long sickle-shaped wings as it hunts down large insects and small birds on the wing. They love dragonflies, so if it's a hot summer's day and you're over marshy moorland, rivers or lakes where insects are going to turn up in numbers, that's where they are going to want to be. Unlike a Peregrine, which is a dive-bomber, a Hobby is more like a dogfighting fighter pilot zeroing in on its enemy's tail. They are well known for catching dragonflies in flight with a single talon, and then they'll soar in a circle while they neatly transfer the dragonfly from their talons to their bill, by lifting their feet right up. It's almost like some sort of yoga move – it's impressive to watch. But maybe even more impressive is the kind of birds that it's able to chase down. These guys can not only catch Skylarks and Starlings – they can chase down Swallows and Swifts, the fastest birds on the planet. And they can sometimes be mistaken for a really large Swift, although they don't have forked tails, but they're sometimes difficult to see when they're moving as quickly as they both do. They do look like Peregrines, but the Hobby has the distinctive rusty red lower belly and vertical streaks on its breast compared to the horizontal bars of the Peregrine. If I was going to categorise the birds in the book by how difficult they are to see, the Hobby would be near the top. You need to be in the right place at the right time. So if you have seen one, give yourself a proper pat on the back.

The Merlin is our smallest bird of prey – actually only a bit bigger than a Thrush. And sometimes it even looks like a Thrush, and that's no mistake. It's actually a really clever hunting strategy. When they're closing the distance towards their prey, suddenly they change their flying style, using shallow, bouncy wingbeats, just like a Mistle Thrush. So if they're seen by their prey, the victim's just thinking, *oh, it's just a Mistle Thrush. Phew!* before bang! They're back in fighter jet mode. It's a bit like Superman suddenly changing back into Clark Kent for a few seconds.

With that in mind, you'd be forgiven for thinking that they're called Merlins for coming up with this deception wizardry, but I'm afraid not. Their name has got nothing to do with the legendary wizard. Sorry! The name comes from an Old French word (and an Old German word before that) just meaning Falcon. What a let down! They're also known as Pigeon Hawks in North America, and their scientific name also translates as Pigeon Hawk. But that's got nothing to do with Hunting Pigeons, which are a bit beyond all but the strongest female Merlins – it's because their flight does look a bit pigeon-like.

They aren't that many breeding Merlins in the UK – only around a thousand. Most nest on the ground (in the UK, anyway) in a shallow scrape among thick heather, but they do also use old crow nests in trees and crevices in cliffs as well. In summer, you're most likely to see Merlins in upland moorland in the north of England, in the north-west of Northern Ireland and far north and west of Scotland. But in the winter, they leave areas of hilly moorland and head to lower areas and the coast. They're joined by Merlins migrating from Iceland in need of a bit more warmth. Merlins are really well-travelled birds, and are found across much of the northern hemisphere. One population breeds across Scandinavia and Russia and these birds travel south to south-west, central, and south-eastern Europe, parts of central Asia and as far as eastern China, South Korea and Japan in winter. There's another population of Merlins who breed in Canada and Alaska, and they head south in winter to California, the southern US, the Caribbean and Central America.

Males and females are coloured quite differently but they both have quite short, pointed wings, a square tail and a small head. Males have blue-grey backs, yellowish-brown chests with thick brown streaks and a black section toward the end of their tail that ends with a white tip. Females are mainly greyish brown and have dark tails with five whitish horizontal bands.

Merlins usually launch their attacks from a low perch, like a conifer tree, a low rock, a pole, or sometimes just on open ground, waiting for the moment to chase down their prey. And when they're pursuing their prey, they'll often be as low as one metre above the ground. One thing they've learned to do, which is seriously impressive, is hunt together in a pair. This behaviour isn't unique to Merlins (Harris Hawks famously do it, several of them hunting like a pack of wolves) but it is unusual, highly intelligent and requires some serious coordination. The technique involves one Merlin flushing the target in the direction of where the other Merlin is waiting to ambush it. Wow!

WHEATEAR

Scientific name: *Oenanthe oenanthe*

Conservation status (UK/Europe): Amber/Near Threatened

In three words: Bold, observant, active

Look out for: Dark bandit mask (less obvious in female), white bum, black T-shape on tail; hopping along grassy ground near rocks

How easy it is to see them: (Summer only) Fairly Easy – they like rocky uplands across mainly northern, Eastern and south-eastern Europe

A male Wheatear looks like a little ninja with its black stripe extending from its beak to the back of its head and its blue-grey cap and shoulders. They're striking-looking visitors to the UK, arriving in spring from tropical Africa and leaving in autumn. There are actually two different races of Wheatear that come to the UK. The first race usually arrives in March (the males turn up before the females) but sometimes as early as late February and stay around the coast until they move inland to breed. A second race, known as the Greenland Wheatear, uses the UK as a pitstop in April before it continues on all the way up to Greenland and northern Canada via Iceland.

You can usually see Wheatears on the ground, on short grass, hopping or running, bowing and bobbing, looking for insects. You'll always find them near rocky areas and they make their nests in tiny underground burrows that they'll shoot in and out of on the hunt for insects, spiders and insect larvae. You can often see them on a rock overlooking grassland while they stand upright, almost arching their backs. When they do fly, they often fly low and just a short distance before going back to their hopping and bobbing or watching you from a rock saying, 'What are you looking at? Why are you so close?!' They don't scare that easy! They can also hover, too, which is pretty impressive.

Their names aren't anything to do with Wheat or Ear, funnily enough. It comes from the Old English for White and Arse, after their very obvious white bums. They're just a bit bigger than a Robin and the tip of their tails forms a black T-shape that extends into the white bum. They've also got sandy orange-coloured breasts. Females have the same coloured breast, but they're more brownish overall, don't have the ninja mask but do have a pale eyestripe over their eyes and the distinctive white bum with the black T-shape on their tails.

In the UK, they're not fans of southern or central England, preferring Wales, Scotland, the Yorkshire Dales, Lake District, North Pennines and Northumberland, although you can find them in south-western England and the Kent coast, near the coast in Northern Ireland and on the west coast of Ireland. The Greenland Wheatear race stay near the coast and will have travelled over 18,000 miles in a year, including 2,000 miles of it over the Atlantic without taking a break!

FARMLAND

Farmland is probably the habitat that has changed the most in the last hundred years. That's meant that some traditionally farmland birds are struggling, but there are some really exciting conservation projects underway and some incredible success stories.

Farmland is where you're going to see a Barn Owl – who doesn't love a Barn Owl (other than, maybe, a vole)? Anyway, if you're walking or driving along the edge of a field around dawn or dusk, keep your eyes peeled if you see a little low-flying white flash, because you might be about to see something really beautiful.

Farmland is also where you're going to hear one of the most remarkable Eurasian birds – the Skylark. I get tired just thinking about how much effort it takes for a Skylark to deliver its song, which feels like it's come from heaven.

The Long-tailed Tit certainly wins the cutest bird award. Not just for its tiny, fluffy, lollipop shape, but also the way that they travel in a family group and experience everything together. The highs, the lows, the squabbling, the comfort, the care, the familiarity. It's like watching a soap opera filming these guys, but it's such a privilege. It's no wonder I often hear people tell me they are their favourite bird. And to be fair, it's a strong choice.

Red Kites have had some highs and lows in their time too, but they are one of the great conservation highlights of the past 35 years since 13 Spanish Red Kites were reintroduced to the Chilterns, north-west of London, in 1990. In a testament to how well that project has gone, Red Kite chicks born in the UK in 2022 have been sent over to Spain to help stop the decline in numbers there. It's incredible to be able to return the favour for our European friends and says a lot about conservation being a common language. We all want to see wonderful birds like the Red Kite thrive.

BARN OWL

Scientific name: *Tyto alba*

Conservation status (UK/Europe): Green/Secure

In three words: Silent, floating spectre

Look out for: A white shape fluttering like a butterfly low over a field edge at dusk or dawn

How easy it is to see them: Challenging

Almost everyone knows what Barn Owls look like, with their white, heart-shaped faces, beautiful mottled golden-buff and grey feathers and snow-white underparts. Its face shape isn't just pretty, though. It's designed to pick up as much sound as possible and funnel it into its ear openings.

Generally, with owls, if you look at the colour of their eyes, you can tell what time of the day they mainly hunt. Golden-orange eyes, like with the Eurasian Eagle Owl, tends to be associated with hunting in the early morning and late evening. Little Owls have greenish eyes, which indicates they hunt all through the day. Barn Owls have black eyes, so you know they're going to be hunting mainly in the night. And while that's true, Barn Owls are also often active at dusk (and sometimes around dawn), so if you're in the country near the edge of a field, you might see one loitering on a fence post, flying low over the ground patrolling for prey, looking like little floating ghosts, or hovering over something that's worth a second look. And in winter and when feeding their young, they do hunt in daylight. They don't like hunting in the rain, though – their feathers are soft and not very waterproof.

So, if you want to see a Barn Owl and it's dawn or dusk, keep a look out at field edges on non-rainy days, if you're walking or driving past. You might see a white flash next to you. Either that, or you might see one on a fence post moving its head to stare at you as you drive past.

It's not quite the same up on the west coast of Scotland. We don't have any ploughed fields here, so we don't really have field edges as such. That just means it's all good hunting territory for a hunting Barn Owl up here.

One thing you won't do is hear a Barn Owl when it's hunting. It doesn't want anything to disturb its prey, so it flies almost silently and quite slowly, with its big broad wings, homing in on an unsuspecting vole, mouse or shrew. It does sometimes hunt birds as well, however, like House Sparrows and Skylarks. But when it does make a noise, wow, does it make a noise. It sounds like a clip from a horror film, with its piercing scream that cuts right through you. They also hiss like a snake to warn you off and snap their beaks. Between those habits and the shriek, it's perhaps no wonder they earned the nickname 'demon owl' or 'screech owl'. It doesn't hoot, though. Not all owls do!

I've learned a lot from Barn Owls. When I moved up to Ardnamurchan, it was one of the first birds I planned to photograph after seeing one come out of an outbuilding. And my patience paid off because I learned how to make nest boxes, where to put them (inside a quiet outbuilding) and what to fill them with (owl pellets, which they use for their nesting material). For an animal that has such pristine white feathers, it's amazing that they live in such filth! They basically like being surrounded by decomposing inedible parts of mice and voles, which they'll flatten out and sit on. Each to their own! Nevertheless, it was such a great feeling when a family moved in. And nest boxes like these are really helping these guys out. Up to 80 per cent of Barn Owls now nest in man-made boxes. That's mainly because the kind of places they traditionally nest in – barns (perhaps unsurprisingly!), farm buildings and ruined or falling apart structures – are more often than not being converted into nice farmhouse extensions and swanky Airbnbs.

I've actually only ever found one 'natural' habitat that Barn Owls are nesting in near me – in the roots of a tree that is connected to a little cliff. I sometimes wonder where Barn Owls would live if we didn't have buildings. It's the same with House Martins! They've adapted to the things that humans have built, and so maybe it's no surprise that they're common throughout Europe (except Scandinavia). You can actually find them on every continent except Antarctica. They're the most widely distributed owl on Earth, so they're doing something right. That being said, seeing as we all seem to be converting some of their nesting locations, I feel like it's only fair that we should be helping out to provide nest boxes for them.

LAPWING

Scientific name: *Vanellus vanellus*

Conservation status (UK/Europe): Red/Threatened

In three words: Black-and-white vocal flock

Look out for: Amazing black head plumes (when on the ground); iridescent greens and blues; ping-pong-bat wings in flight

How easy it is to see them: Fairly Easy – they breed in uplands and head to lowlands in winter where they form large flocks

There's a lot to love for the Lapwing. It's got style, that's for sure. The first thing to say is a Lapwing looks beautiful whether it's up close or in flight. From afar, you might encounter a big flock of them over farmland in winter and they might just look like monochrome black and white, but there's a lot more going on. Firstly, it's not really black. It shimmers with iridescent greens and purples, like a Magpie, which is why it's sometimes known as the Green Plover. It has these extraordinarily round wings that look more like they belong to an Owl rather than a wading bird and it has this remarkable, wispy dark crest that extends well above its head and looks like it belongs on a Bird of Paradise.

They're also known as 'Pee-Wits' because they make a distinctive two-syllable sound that sounds a bit like that. Although, saying that, other languages interpret this noise in very different ways (a bit like 'cock-a-doodle-doo' is *kikeriki* in German and *gaggalago* in Icelandic). In German, the sound a Lapwing makes is *kiebitz* or *vivak* in Croatian. Francis Orpen Morris, the 19th-century reverend/naturalist and author, said it was like 'the puffing of the engine of a railway-train, heard at some distance', which I liked. I think it sounds more like a broken police siren.

The origin of the name Lapwing is a bit harder to get to the bottom of. It's possible it comes from the Old English word 'hleapewince' which means 'to leap with a flicker in it', which makes sense if you've ever seen a Lapwing flock in flight. But then again, 'Lapwing' might refer to the 'lapping' noise its big, rounded wings make as it flies. Or 'Lapwing' could refer to the defence tactic parent Lapwings use, by pretending they've got a broken wing to lure predators away from their nests. That's why a group of Lapwings is known as a 'deceit', by the way. To be honest, I like each of these three potential origin stories, so pick your favourite.

And then there's the display flight of the male. Wow! It normally flies in this floppy sort of fashion, but in spring when it's trying to attract a mate, it comes out with this tumbling, cartwheeling, and sometimes frankly suicidal-looking feat of aerobatics. It's like they've suddenly become dogfighting old fighter planes or something. But they're not only fighting with each other to win a female, they're also fighting the landscape. That takes fearlessness. And that extends to the female, too. I've seen tractors pulling ploughs through a field and a female Lapwing will stand up to it. A bit like the famous protestor standing up to the tank. And the farmer sees the Lapwing and lifts the plough over the ground so it won't hit her, but she doesn't know that! She'd happily die trying to protect her little ones. Incredible. Heart of a lioness.

Most birds have one distinctive feature that sets them apart. A Lapwing has about a dozen. Which is

why we need to do what we can to help them, because
as with a few of the other farmland birds we've talked
about, Lapwings are on the Red List, and for much the
same reason.

LONG-TAILED TIT

Scientific name: *Aegithalos caudatus*
Conservation status (UK/Europe): Green/Secure
In three words: Fluffy, communicative, family-orientated
Look out for: Delicate, little black-and-white lollipops
bouncing through the air in family groups
How easy it is to see them: Fairly Easy – they travel
together and return to the same place each night

The Long-tailed Tit is a beautiful little bird with a dainty beak, an incredible long flowing tail and the sweetest little twittering call. Their tails are actually longer than their little plump bodies, which makes them look a bit like lollipops. They're almost like a kind of Disney-cartoon version of a sweet little bird, to be honest. They fly around in family groups and you often hear them all making their little 'peeping' calls at the same time and if one of them gets into trouble for any reason, they all stay behind and try and help out.

When we ring them, instead of releasing them one at a time like we do with most other species, we wait until they've all been ringed and then release them at the same time as a family group. And afterwards, they'll end up flying off to a tree together, sitting close to each other, peep to each other and all I can think is they're all chatting to each other saying, *Is everyone here, Is everyone ok? OK let's move on!* And then when the sun's coming down, they'll all roost together in a line, all facing the same way on the same branch to keep warm, and they'll come back to that same branch every night. They're creatures of habit! If you ever find that place where they roost, it's so special because you can wait there quietly, watching their little family bedtime routine. There's a hierarchy going on, though, so the more senior family members get the warm spots in the middle, so you'll see them gently jostling for position until everyone's in the right place. It's amazing to watch, like a sweet little soap opera involving mums, dads, aunties, uncles and kids. Survival is a long-term family thing for the Long-tailed Tit and that's unusual for birds – it's the kind of behaviour you associate with chimpanzees and other really smart primates.

Their domed nests are a thing of beauty, taking up to a month of finding moss and lichen, which is all stuck together using spiders' webs (known as gossamer) and lined with feathers (sometimes up to 2,000). The fact that they use spider's silk means that it can expand as the chicks inside grow. They build them in hedgerows, brambles and other dense, low vegetation.

They're among the smallest and lightest of UK birds, weighing about the same as a 10p piece. And the great news is that their numbers have been steadily increasing since the 1980s (except for a decrease recorded in the 'Big Garden Birdwatch' in 2022, which I'm hoping is just a blip).

RED KITE

Scientific name: *Milvus milvus*

Conservation status (UK/Europe): Green/Secure

In three words: Slow, floating glider

Look out for: Long, pale forked tail moving like a rudder; reddy brown body; a large gliding bird that looks like a kite!

How easy it is to see them: Fairly Easy over southern England and Wales, western Spain, south-west and eastern France

Seeing Red Kites over west London was a big surprise
to me when I came down to London for *Strictly*. These
guys are a big conservation success story, but it's worth
going into the journey they've taken over the past few
centuries, because they've had quite a time of it. In the
1400s, Red Kites were basically considered a public
service, helping to keep the streets clean by making off
with rotting food, rubbish and rodents. They were so well
thought of that they were protected by a royal decree,
which meant that you could be executed for killing a kite.
But then their fortunes fell massively.

   After a series of poor harvests and all kinds of horrible
diseases appearing or reappearing, King Henry VIII
(who wasn't exactly known for compassion) passed a law
called the Preservation of Grain Act in 1532. Under this
law, which might as well have been called the *Persecution
of Wildlife Act*, Kites, along with Crows, Owls, badgers,
bats, hedgehogs and, amazingly, Kingfishers, were all
classified as 'vermin'. And even worse than that, you'd
receive a bounty for each of these animals you killed,
ranging from one penny to 12 pence, which was a lot
when you bear in mind that most people earned about
four pence a day. This law had huge consequences for
wildlife in England, pushing some species to the edge of
extinction, and a lot of it was based on superstition and
well, rubbish, really. Hedgehogs were thought to drink
milk straight from cows' udders while they lay down at

night! You wonder how these kinds of stories started, particularly given that we now know that hedgehogs are lactose intolerant, which is why you shouldn't leave milk out for them.

Anyway, back to our poor Red Kites, who in Tudor times were thought to both spread disease (which wasn't true – if anything they helped reduce it by eating carrion) and steal grain (again not true because it has never been part of their diet). Fast forward to the 19th century and they're not faring much better. This time they're being targeted by gamekeepers who thought they hunted game (again, not true), but this time their numbers declined hugely. By 1871, they were extinct in England and had disappeared from Scotland by 1879. There were a few surviving birds in Wales, but we're talking a handful of them. By the 1980s, Red Kites were one of only three globally threatened species in the UK.

But then in 1986, the RSPB and the NCC (Nature Conservancy Council) discussed an exciting plan to reintroduce them. And then, between 1989 and 1994, 93 Red Kites from Sweden and Spain were released at two sites – one on the Black Isle, in the Scottish Highlands, and the other in Buckinghamshire. They started breeding three years later, at both sites. Now I can see them flying over my parents' place in Northampton! You'd think there'd be nothing for them to eat, but they're scavengers and are pretty resourceful at finding where the grub's at.

A Red Kite is a good instance of the bird's name giving you quite a bit to go on when you're trying to identify them. They have red-brown bodies and their deeply forked large, triangular tail does look like a kite. You'll often see them soaring above roads in the west of England, sometimes coming only a few feet above the terrain so you can often get a really good look at these incredibly graceful, beautiful birds of prey. They also live year-round across the western half of Spain, eastern France and parts of southern Italy, and they breed in Germany, Poland, eastern Denmark and southern Sweden.

SKYLARK

Scientific name: *Alauda arvensis*

Conservation status (UK/Europe): Red/Least Concern

In three words: Chattery, energetic performer

Listen out for: Incredibly beautiful unbroken song delivered high up over fields

How easy it is to see them: Fairly Easy – but if you hear the song, get the binos out and sit back (don't stare at the sun!)

These guys sing from the heavens. It's that wonderful. It's a musical, constantly rising, falling, dancing, endless variable excitable warble that can last upwards of 15 minutes. They just sound so happy! And that's why the word for a group of Skylarks is 'an exaltation'.

The male usually sings while he's hovering, rising and falling. When you hear it, I think people assume they're just a few feet over your head and get frustrated when you can't hear who's responsible for this joyful outpouring! That's because they're actually at least 50 metres up, which means the song travels far and wide to broadcast to nearby rivals and attract females, because what they're really saying through their song is: 'Pick me! I can sing louder, higher and for longer than everyone else!' And the females, who will be on the ground, are listening and judging which of the males is the strongest and the fittest, and they'll do that based on how loud they sing and how long they can go on for.

When the males finally come down from their song flight (they must be absolutely knackered!), they do this beautiful parachuting manoeuvre, still singing all the time, where they fold their wings in and drop towards the ground before reopening their wings, and fanning their tail to suddenly cushion their landing. It reminds me of a gymnast pulling off a dismount, lifting their arms up and going 'Ta-dah'!

You will need to get your binoculars out if you have them because they can be nigh on impossible to spot with the naked eye – we are talking well over 50 metres a lot of the time. Chris Packham (wildlife TV presenter and conservationist) gave me the idea that, once you can hear a Skylark, you find a comfy spot and sit back with your binos on until you locate it. It can take a while, especially on a cloudless day when you've got no reference points in the sky, but it's worth it, trust me. Then just sit back and enjoy one of nature's miracles! Because you'll catch the whole thing, the parachuting down and dismount. What a performance!

If you haven't got a pair of binoculars with you and you're lucky, you might be able to see a Skylark singing from a fence post, a wall or a big rock. They'll sing through spring and summer, but you can also hear them on clear winter days, too, which is a lovely bonus when you're out for a walk. If you do catch sight of one, it's about halfway between the size of a thrush and sparrow and looks about halfway between the two as well, with its streaked chest (which stops suddenly before it gets to the bird's belly) and chestnut-brown wings, which are short but wide and triangular-looking in flight. It's also got a streaked crest that rises up when it's alert or excited, which both makes it look really pretty but also helps to identify it. Also, on the ground, Skylarks quite often crouch down, assuming a kind of anxious 'brace' position, which is another helpful distinguishing feature.

The Skylark has been placed on the Red List in the UK due to the rapid decline in numbers. This is thought to be to do with the change in the time farmers sow cereals, from spring to autumn. This means that the seeds and weed leaves that Skylarks eat over winter are much more scarce, and it also means that when it comes to their breeding season, the autumn-sown crops are then too tall and dense for Skylarks to nest in. One solution is to create 'Skylark plots', which are 4-metre by 4-metre bare areas in fields, (away from field edges and telegraph poles), that Skylarks can forage in. These areas have been shown to only have a tiny effect on a farmer's yield. The idea was pioneered by the RSPB in the late 1990s and, thanks to its success, the UK government now rewards farmers who provide Skylark plots on their farms. They don't just help Skylarks, though. Yellowhammers are also benefitting. Everyone's a winner!

WAXWING

Scientific name: *Bombycilla garrulus*
Conservation status (UK/Europe): Green/Secure
In three words: Stunning, confident, hungry
Look out for: Amazing pinkish pointed crest; black
bandit mask; yellow-tipped tail
How easy it is to see them: (Winter only): Challenging –
look out for flocks near berry trees

I love these guys – they're the beautiful 'caped crusaders' of the bird world. I had a tiny garden in Bangor when I was at university and a bird I'd never seen before landed. I took a picture and sent it to my friend, and my phone absolutely blew up. Suddenly, lots of people turned up at my door to try and see the waxwing that was perched there! I love thinking that my garden, wherever it is I am, is home to not only the garden birds that live there all year round, but also birds that might have come from Europe, Russia or the Arctic, like the Waxwing, which is a special winter migrant. And it's another great reason to go birding in the winter, because you do get some unusual, stunning visitors, and with the lack of leaves on the trees, it does make it easier to see them too.

Waxwings are stunning birds with their incredible colours and beautiful pointed crests, which they use for courtship. Like Redwings, who also visit in winter. They love rowan and hawthorn bushes and can eat up to 1,000 berries in a single day! If there's a problem with the berry crop in Continental Europe and Russia, usually because the weather is well below freezing, large numbers of Waxwings will fly to the UK. It happens every few years – in 2012–3, Waxwings turned up everywhere there was a rowan tree in large flocks. We're talking supermarket car parks, new housing developments, playparks – everywhere! It ended up being called a 'Waxwing Winter'. And they'll happily eat berries from a tree right in front of you. They're not skittish birds. If you put a broken apple half on a stick in your garden, you can attract them, and they'll happily eat it four metres away from you.

They're called Waxwings because they have bright red tips to their secondary feathers (the set of inner flight feathers on their wings) that look like drops of wax that you can imagine using to seal a letter in Medieval times. You can't mistake them for anything else really, with their orangey pink bodies, black ninja mask and bright yellow band at the end of the tail. They're about the size of a Starling and they'll brighten up your day when you see one. Unless that is, you tell everyone and then the entire neighbourhood is at your door!

YELLOWHAMMER

Scientific name: *Emberiza citrinella*

Conservation status (UK/Europe): Red/Least Concern

In three words: Energetic, flashy, chatty

Look out for: A bird with a bright yellow head and streaked brown breast singing at the top of a gorse bush or hedge

How easy it is to see them: Fairly Easy in open countryside across the UK and northern Europe. Look for the gorse!

The cheerful call of this colourful little bird, amazingly, sounds like 'little bit of bread, no cheese', which the author Enid Blyton (who wrote the Famous Five and the Secret Seven series of books) helped to popularise in her work. And they literally call all day, to the point where you wonder where they find the energy. They do like the limelight, as well, singing proudly from the top of a hedge, bush or fence and not being that interested in moving unless you get really close. Males have an unmistakable bright-yellow head, streaked breasts and reddish-brown wings. Females and young ones are a bit paler, but they've still got enough yellow on their heads and faces, along with dark streaks on their breasts to identify them. There are some similar-looking birds around, though, like the Wood Warbler, who comes over in summer, but when you know the 'little bit of bread, no cheese call', it's so useful as a platform to either identify a Yellowhammer, or rule it out.

In winter, they become sociable and get together in big flocks with other birds. Although they're still common on farmland in the UK and across northern, central and Eastern Europe, Australia and New Zealand – where they were brought over in the 1860s and 1870s. This wasn't for sentimental reasons to remind people of home, but as part of a plan to help control the number of insects which were affecting farmers' crops; although this plan backfired because Yellowhammers actually only go for insects when they're breeding. The rest of the time they like seeds, which definitely didn't end up endearing them to farmers.

It is a funny name for a bird, I grant you. 'Yellow' is fair enough but where does the 'hammer' come from? It doesn't hammer anything with its beak or make a noise like a hammer. To get to the origin, you have to go back all the way to William the Conqueror. After he invaded, the Anglo-Saxon language slowly began to change, incorporating parts of William's language – Norman-French – to create a new language which eventually became known as Middle English. Dandelion is a good example of this. It's actually an adapted version of the French *dent-de-lion*, which means lion's tooth, referring to the jagged shape the plant's leaves have. So 'dandelion' became the new, user-friendly version. Some birds' names also changed along similar lines, like the Yellowhammer. It was called the Yellow Ammer (with 'Ammer' originally coming from the German word for a bunting – small, ground-dwelling, seed-eating sparrow-like birds). OK, history lesson done for the day.

Sadly, although these guys are common to the UK, they're actually in serious decline, earning them a place on the Red List. Their population numbers fell by 58 per cent between 1970 and 2016. That's mainly due to changing land use, pesticides, and the fact that there aren't as many seeds available for them on farmland.

While they're considered of 'Least Concern' in Europe, their numbers are also declining. It's better news on my side of the border, in Scotland, though, where their numbers have been increasing. That might well be partly down to the amazing conservation efforts in parts of Scotland by farmers, land managers and volunteers to try and save the related Corn Bunting, which has seen record increases in numbers and brought it back from the brink!

RIVERS, MARSHES AND ESTUARIES

You'll find two of the most incredible, beautiful birds in the whole of the UK and northern Europe close to rivers and streams: the Kingfisher and the Dipper. Although I have to admit that the Kingfisher has been a bogey bird for me. Every birder has one bird that somehow eludes them, however hard they try! And I'd wanted to see this sparkling little jewel of a bird all my life, but somehow, it never quite happened. That was until 2021. What a year, and what a bird! The Dipper I've got to know (and admire) very well because I've spent a fair bit of time with them on bird-ringing trips. What they can do and how they have evolved to do it is just mind-blowing.

Marshes and estuaries are two of the places where you'll encounter 'waders' – a loose group of around 200 long-legged birds that wade out into water looking mainly for aquatic insects, crustaceans, worms and molluscs. They're also found along coastlines (and are known as 'shorebirds' rather than 'waders' in the US), but I've chosen to focus on the ones that you tend to find in marshy environments. Waders have specialised and often very distinctive beaks to scoop up their prey, like Curlews, Snipe and Oystercatchers, with their bright-orange beaks making them particularly identifiable. Some even have beaks that curve upwards, like the Avocet, which uses it to filter through wet mud for crustaceans and worms.

CURLEW

Scientific name: *Numenius arquata*

Conservation status (UK/Europe): Red/Near Threatened

In three words: Large, long-billed wader

Listen/look out for: Mournful two-toned call; look out for long legs, a long, downward-curved bill and a small head

How easy it is to see them: Fairly Easy around estuaries, more so in winter

The Curlew gets its name from the call it makes, which is a two-note, rising 'cur-lee' sound, and it's one of the most incredible calls in the animal world. I can hear these guys from my window in Ardnamurchan and it's always such a joy. It's the sound of home. To me they sound angelic, although a lot of people find the call haunting or sorrowful, like the birds are lost or need help. Not my Scottish mother Amanda, though, who thinks it's one of the most incredible sounds on Earth and one that she remembers so fondly growing up as a child near Aberdeen. But it's not her favourite bird – that's the Whooper Swan, which she's told me she wants to come back as in another life because she likes their long-distance travelling and the fact they travel in family groups. I love that she tells me these things and that birds have now had such a lovely effect on her life!

I get that their song sounds quite melancholy because it always feels like it's far off and lonesome, like they've somehow lost their partner and are calling, 'I'm over here, can you hear me?' I've learned their whistling call in flight and can actually divert a Curlew to fly past me, which is such a privilege because I see them from really close and has enabled me to take some fantastic shots of them from just outside my door. I've got this little pond and the shore is maybe 30 metres away and I can see them moving around ahead. One time, I got one step too close and they all started calling. They are so beautiful in flight. They are one of my favourite birds in the world, that's for sure. I think it's because they remind me of home, the life I've built there and the incredible people I've been lucky enough to meet.

Curlews are strange-looking birds the first time you really see one. You tend to find yourself asking, *why is your beak almost the same length as the rest of your body?! How is that beneficial for anything?!*

As soon as they land, they blend in so well with their surroundings, with their mottled browns and greys, and it's only when they move that you notice its silhouettes and its long, gorgeous beak that's bent ever so gently, with the tip just about pointing towards the ground. I always wonder how Curlews preen themselves but they manage to keep their feathers so pristine and beautiful.

The Curlew is actually the largest wader we have in Europe – they're roughly the same size as a female pheasant. Young Curlews feed on insects and spiders, while the adults go for earthworms, beetles, caterpillars, spiders and cranefly larvae. They can be seen around the UK coastline, but their numbers continue to decline, so much so that they were put on the Red List in 2015 and remain there. While they breed in a number of different habitats, they prefer moorlands, rough grasslands and bogs, which is why they've suffered from changing land use, especially the drainage of moorland and farmland and the modification of agricultural grassland.

Both components of its Latin name, *Numenius arquata* (which really does sound like a spell out of Harry Potter), refer to the shape of its bill. 'Numenius' comes from the Greek words 'Neos' and 'Mene', meaning New Moon, which is crescent-shaped. And 'arquata' is Latin for a bow used in archery, which is also curved. Gotta love a good fact!

DIPPER

Scientific name: *Cinclus cinclus*

Conservation status (UK/Europe): Amber/Unknown

In three words: Powerful, vigilant, aquatic-specialist

Look out for: The white bib contrasting with dark head and back; cocked tail; body bobbing up and down; slipping in and out of water

How easy it is to see them: Challenging – search around fast-flowing upland rivers

I learned to remember the Latin name for a Dipper, which is *Cinclus cinclus*, because Dippers sink, but then they always pop back up again, so they are 'Sink-less'. You've got to do something with your time when you're waiting and watching for birds! The first thing to say about the Dipper (other than that Latin name diversion) is that it's a unique, amazing bird that really doesn't look like it should be able to do the things that it does. With its pure-white throat and breast, contrasting with its smart chocolate-brown back and wings, it looks a bit like a very smartly dressed, short, stout and excitable waiter.

Look for these little gems by fast-flowing rivers in hills and mountains all over Wales, in the north of England (the Peak District and Lake District are good spots) the Borders and in the Highlands, and in lowland rivers in the south-west of England (Devon and Somerset). They're always bobbing their tails up and down and cocking their tails, like a wren, and you'll often see them sitting on a rock or standing and probing in the water. Their song is high pitched, and that's because it cuts through the dull, drumming sound of the fast-flowing water so they can communicate with each other. Clever stuff. And if they can't hear each other, they'll be able to see the bobbing and the obvious white bib.

It's called a Dipper because it dips into the water to catch insect larvae, small fish, fish eggs, tiny crustaceans and molluscs. But the word 'Dipper' sells it massively short because it does a lot more than that. Not only does it walk through fast-flowing water (which is pretty impressive when you weigh between 50 and 75 grams), it can actually walk underwater along the riverbed against the current. It gets there with its strong wings, that are really more like flippers than wings. And unlike other songbirds, which have hollow bones, the dipper's bones are solid, which helps reduce their buoyancy. It stays on the riverbed thanks to its powerful claws that work a bit like a mountaineer's crampons. Its feathers are waterproof thanks to an oil-producing gland at the base of its tail, and you can see it shake off little beads of water when it emerges from the water. It means, when they're underwater, they have this slightly ghostly slivery shimmer to them. A Dipper also has a specialised nasal flap to stop water going up its nostrils. We could all do with that! They've also got specialised focus muscles in their eyes that change the curvature of their lens to help them see underwater. And then there's its blood, which has been shown to contain high levels of haemoglobin, which means it can store oxygen when it's diving so it can remain underwater for over half a minute.

I've studied Dippers up close because I used to ring them in North Wales. I realised that at night, Dippers fly up into the underside of bridges and roost there. I've been there, with a camera and a flashlight, shining it at them and they won't move. They'll look at you but won't be flustered at all because they know they can't see well enough to fly away. I suppose there's no need to panic when you can't do anything about it! So it was easy enough to pick each of them up, place a ring on them, put the flashlight back on and place them back down exactly where they were. No harm done.

Dippers are very good indicators of how clean a river is. If you can see a Dipper, it means the river is well-oxygenated enough to support the things it most likes to eat – caddis larvae and mayfly larvae. While there's really good news that the Dipper has returned to urban rivers in South Wales in the last 35 years (after improvements in the treatment of waste and the regulation of toxic chemicals helped clean up our rivers), pollutants are still being found in Dipper eggs. A study carried out by Cardiff University (published in 2014) showed that urban Dippers were hatching underweight chicks compared with Dippers in rural areas, and were hatching fewer female chicks. So, there's still a long way to go to make our rivers clean and safe enough to support these beautiful creatures.

GREAT CRESTED GREBE

Scientific name: *Podiceps cristatus*

Conservation status (UK/Europe): Green/Secure

In three words: Elegant, spectacular dancer

Look out for: A streamlined duck with a long neck, neck ruff and dark crest

How easy it is to see them: Fairly Easy, if you're near a slow-moving lowland lake or reservoir

This bird was always going to squeeze into this book because of all the birds in the UK, the Great Crested Grebe is the most likely to win *Strictly Come Dancing* (as I'll explain in a minute). And, boy, what a looker it is too. Plus, they were nearly hunted to extinction, which is a story that helped found the RSPB. But now they're back, pretty widespread, and if you know where to look, you'll most probably find one. This entry has got it all going on!

So, what's a grebe, then? It's a diving waterbird (not a duck) that you'll see in lakes and rivers mostly across central and southern England, Ireland, France, Spain, The Netherlands and Belgium. As bird families go, Grebes are pretty stunning. The Great Crested Grebe has a long, elegant neck, a slender head tapering into a dagger-like bill, beautiful dark head plumes that extend upwards and a dark orange ruff with black tips around its neck that, when it's extended, looks a bit like a lion's mane. The Great Crested Grebe is perfectly designed for a life catching fish underwater. It looks a bit awkward on land, with its feet set quite far back. In winter, its plumage is mostly white and dark grey and it loses its ruff.

The Great Crested Grebe might not even be the most stunning of the Grebes we get in the UK. That award might just go to the Slavonian Grebe, with its golden ear tufts, black upperparts and chestnut underparts. It's one of our rarest nesting birds and the place to see it is the stunning Loch Ruthven near the northern end of Loch Ness, which has a superstar cast, including Ospreys and Black-throated Divers.

The Great Crested Grebe's plumage is so beautiful that it was popularly used in fashionable ladies' hats and various other accessories in the early 19th century. By 1860, there were only around a hundred birds left. This grebe wasn't the only UK bird to suffer this way – Kingfishers, Herons and Owls were also hunted as well as birds from around the world like Hummingbirds and Birds of Paradise. Up stepped a remarkable lady, Emily Williamson, who wrote to the British Ornithologists Union urging them to do something about it. But they ignored her.

Undeterred, from her home in Didsbury (just south of Manchester), she set up the Plumage League in 1889. Its main aim was to end the trade in feathers for fashion. And to this end, Emily joined forces with another pioneering lady, Eliza Phillips, who had formed the group Fur, Fin and Feather Folk in Croydon, south London. Together, they founded the Society for the Protection of Birds in 1889. Ten years later, they had 20,000 members and people in power were starting to take notice, including Queen Victoria, who, that same year, stopped military regiments from using Osprey feathers. The organization was awarded a royal charter in 1904 and became the Royal Society for the Protection of Birds (RSPB). And through the hard work of the RSPB's founders, overcoming all sorts of obstacles including indifference and cartoons in publications like *Punch* mocking the importance of the cause they were fighting for, they attracted the attention of the influential Duchess of Portland, who became the RSPB's first president. By 1908, the Plumage Bill was presented to Parliament but didn't go any further. Another attempt happened in 1914, but the start of the First World War stopped it in its tracks again. Then, in 1919, Nancy Astor became the first woman MP to take her seat in the House of Commons (women had only won the right to vote in 1918, and even then it was restricted to women over 30 who owned property; the same year women over 21 were able to stand for election as an MP) and she steered the Plumage Prohibition Bill through parliament. And on 1 July 1921, the Plumage Act made it illegal to import bird feathers. Largely thanks to the remarkable work of three women.

The courtship dance of the Great Crested Grebe has to be seen to be believed. The first time I saw one, it felt like something I should be paying to watch. It's a magical spectacle, and happens in spring. The first part involves a head-shaking display with crest and ruff extended, while the pair faces each other, which seems like a greeting gesture, because they probably will have paired up on their wintering grounds, but won't have travelled to their breeding grounds together.

Then we've got synchronised swimming, bill-dipping, preening and the pièce de résistance, the 'penguin dance'. Both birds dive slowly together to collect water weed in their beaks, then swim back to the surface, rise up in the water while holding their heads low, close to the water's surface. Then the pair meet, rear up out of the water so they're upright, frantically paddling all the time. It's just a few seconds long, but wow, what a performance! Tens all round.

GREY HERON

Scientific name: *Ardea cinerea*

Conservation status (UK/Europe): Green/Secure

In three words: Tall, solitary, statuesque

Look out for: A big grey, looming, long-legged bird with a pointy beak skulking around the edges of ponds and lakes

How easy it is to see them: Really Easy

You can usually see a Heron standing silently and motionlessly at the edge of a pond, river, lake or marsh, looking like something out of *Jurassic Park*. At the same time, though, they're strangely elegant, with their long necks, ash-grey backs and black eyestripe ending in narrow, black neck plumes. They use their long, strong legs to lurk in the water, waiting patiently for the right moment to strike or wade through shallow water hunting for prey, bending their long necks in an S-shape, which they'll straighten to instantly catch some unfortunate fish, amphibian or small mammal (rats, mice, moles, even weasels!) with their spear-like bills. They've even learned to dip rats and mice in the water to soften them before swallowing it head-first so the grain of the fur points downwards. Lovely! Although, having said that, I imagine they will have had to learn this skill the hard way because Herons are known for trying to swallow prey that is way too big for them.

You don't really appreciate quite how large they are until they fly over you with their looping, slightly lumbering wingbeats (although they can be a lot quicker when they want to), their necks coiled in and their yellow legs dangling behind them. They're up to a metre long, often with a wingspan of over 2 metres (which is about the same as a smaller Golden Eagle, by the way). Plus, like a Golden Eagle, they can live up to around 25 years.

These magnificent birds were actually hunted in the 15–17th centuries by trained Peregrine Falcons and Hawks. Peregrines, which weigh a lot less than a Grey Heron, were used to catch them in the air, not always successfully. If the Heron got the upper hand during the aerial combat and rose above the Falcon, it would sometimes take the opportunity to poo on the Falcon, which would then give up the pursuit! From what I've been able to uncover, the Peregrines and Hawks wouldn't actually kill the Herons, they would drop them near the ground (almost completely uninjured) and then the falconer would intervene. Sadly, though, Herons were a delicacy at royal banquets and were still being eaten (although rarely) until at least the 19th century.

Grey Herons usually nest in treetops, and contrary to an old urban legend, they don't dig out two holes for their feet so they can sit in the nest with their legs dangling down! They head for the trees to steer clear of predators because while the adults are apex predators, their young are vulnerable to birds of prey, and even otters if the nest is on the ground.

Some members of the Heron family have learned fiendish ways to catch their prey. The Black Heron (native to Sub-Saharan Africa and Madagascar) uses its wings like an umbrella to cast a dark shadow over the water to attract fish. It's a technique called 'canopy feeding' and I remember David Attenborough talking about it in *The Life of Birds.* Several herons, including the Green Heron (native to North and Central America) have been recorded using bread as bait to entice fish to have a nibble before ambushing them. Talk about catch of the day!

GREY WAGTAIL

Scientific name: *Motacilla cinerea*

Conservation status (UK/Europe): Amber/Secure

In three words: Bouncy, skittish, stream-dweller

Look out for: Lemon-yellow flank and underparts; long tail; grey back; Robin-sized

How easy it is to see them: Challenging – look around streams

Wagtails manage to look graceful, elegant and joyful, flitting about low to the ground and constantly bouncing their tails. The trouble with the name 'wagtail' is that it doesn't really match what they do. 'Wag' makes you think they move their tails from side to side, like a dog, but Wagtails actually bounce their tails up and down. Also, as I mentioned earlier, 'Grey Wagtail' doesn't really do justice to this beautiful little bird because it's distinguishing feature is its lemon-yellow breast, belly and rump. But we can't call them Yellow Wagtails, because that name is already taken by the Yellow Wagtail, which is *more* yellow than the Grey Wagtail. Maybe Yellow-bellied Bounce Tail would work better.

There are three species of Wagtail in the UK. The Pied Wagtail, you've probably seen darting across a car park or pavement in a town or city, moving its feet so quickly you can barely even see them before it stops and frantically pumps its tail up and down. They're black and white, widespread, common, here the whole year-round, and they have a two-note call that sounds like 'Chis–ick', which is why Bill Oddie (birder, conservationist, presenter, comedian, musician and writer among other things) calls the Pied Wagtail the 'Chiswick Flyover'!

Yellow Wagtails are summer visitors to the UK, mostly to central and eastern England where they'll arrive in April and May and stay until September when they'll make the long flight to sub-Saharan Africa. They're pretty spectacular looking birds, with bright yellow from throat to tail with mostly yellow faces and olive-green backs. It's got a shorter tail than both the Grey Wagtail and Pied Wagtail and you'll find them mostly in wet meadows, pastures where livestock are grazing, and river valleys. There aren't that many of them, though – only around 20,000 travel here, and their numbers have been falling quickly, so much so that they're another species on the UK Red List.

You'll find Grey Wagtails near fast-flowing rivers and streams in hilly areas all over England, Scotland, Wales, Northern Ireland and Ireland in summer. They move to a much wider range of habitats in winter, but tend to head to lowland areas near water, which can be anything from a farmyard, canal, riverbank, drainage ditch, coastal marsh, garden and even around the roofs and gutters of city buildings. Breeding males have a black throat, which females don't have, and the females are a paler, patchier yellow. Grey Wagtails have much longer tails than the other two Wagtails and they look generally longer and sleeker than the Pied and Yellow. They're not that common – there are only around 37,000 breeding pairs, but encouragingly, they were moved from the Red List to the Amber List in 2021 after their numbers began to increase. Amazing!

All Wagtails like running about on the ground, bouncing their tails up and down and eating insects, but the Pied Wagtail has become more adapted to city life, hoovering up seeds, nuts and scraps in winter. So why do Wagtails wag/bounce their tails? The best theory (I think, anyway) is that it tells potential predators that it's alert and won't miss a trick, which explains why they seem to pump their tails more when a bird of prey is around. Their flight pattern is almost as bouncy as the way they move their tails. And all this movement is why the Latin name for the Wagtail genus is *Motacilla*, which translates as 'little mover'.

Grey Wagtails and Dippers (see page 201) are found in the same habitat, so you'll sometimes see them together, which is a treat, because they're both beautiful little birds with uniquely endearing traits. There have even been cases of Grey Wagtail parents feeding Dipper chicks!

KINGFISHER

Scientific name: *Alcedo atthis*

Conservation status (UK/Europe): Green/Secure

In three words: Colourful, patient fisherman

Look out for: A blue, bullet-like flash down the middle of a slow-moving stream, coming to a stop on a low, overhanging perch

How easy it is to see them: Challenging – it took me years, but I got seriously unlucky! If you wait patiently in the right area, you'll likely see one

I saw a Kingfisher in 2021 for the first time. It's taken me 15 years of looking for them and I figured this is going to be my bogey bird that I never end up seeing. The kind of bird where you turn up to a place hoping to see one and you run into a couple of people who say 'Ah, you should have been here two minutes ago – let me show you my picture!' I'm always happy for them, but also slightly infuriated. I've heard kingfishers a zillion times but last year, I was near Bristol with my friend Rowan Aitchinson (a fellow cameraman) and son of John Aitchinson, one of the most amazing wildlife cameramen ever. Rowan started talking to me about Kingfishers and I said 'Oh, don't get me started on kingfishers!' and he told me that there was a place nearby that he sees them all the time. So we went there together. I didn't even take my binoculars because I was convinced we weren't going to see one. And then, Rowan suddenly said, 'There's one!' and I thought he was winding me up at first. But after I realised he was being serious, and it was just around the bend in the river, I stepped down this muddy bank, teetering on one foot, but it was worth it, because I saw it through John's binoculars for maybe 30 seconds before it darted off. As I clambered back up to solid ground, I thought, *I can die a happy man now!* I got back home and Tweeted about it, so excited. I did get quite a few funny comments from people, saying things like: 'Hamza, you've travelled around the world and seen polar bears and king penguins, leopards and leopard seals but you've never seen a Kingfisher?! We like your style!' I was gutted not to see one until that point, but the feeling I got seeing one was just incredible.

The first thing people tell me when they've seen a kingfisher is how much smaller they are than they thought. They're only just over 15cm long. You mostly see them on low-hanging branches next to slow-moving rivers and lakes where they'll wait for small fish and little aquatic insects and then fly quickly and low over the water to catch them using their oversized, pointy bills before returning to their perch to eat it. Just before they hit the water, they close their eyes, which are protected by a transparent eyelid. The water can't be too fast-flowing or polluted as it won't contain enough fish. Colour-wise, they're one of the more spectacular birds in Britain and northern Europe, with their blue heads and wings contrasting with their bright orange breast. Seeing them in slow motion is even more spectacular.

We've only got one species of kingfisher in Britain and Europe, which is pretty poor representation if you ask me, seeing as there are 114 different species around the world.

They usually choose a vertical river or streambank formed from sandy soil and start excavating a little burrow. The adults feed their young in a unique, highly civilised way compared with other birds, where it's a bit of a free-for-all at grub time. Kingfishers feed each chick in turn, who then move towards the back of the nest to eat. A proper queueing system!

OSPREY

Scientific name: *Pandion haliaetus*
Conservation status (UK/Europe): Amber/Secure
In three words: Observant, gull-like fisherman
Look out for: (when perched) Dark bandit-like mask on pale head; pale underparts, dark wings; in flight: striped tail and possibly carrying a large fish in its talons!
How easy it is to see them: Challenging – you'll need to travel to specific sites to see them in the UK and Europe; can be easily confused with a gull in flight

Seeing an Osprey plunge-dive towards the water's surface with wings half-folded before it throws its talons forward at the last second, and expertly snatching a fish as big as a salmon, is an amazing sight. It looks like it's been choreographed. I remember seeing it for the first time on a David Attenborough documentary as a kid, but I had no idea that this magnificent bird of prey could be found in the UK. But it wasn't always the case. Ospreys, also known as the Sea Hawk and Fish Hawk, were extinct in the British Isles by 1916. But 38 years later, something amazing happened. Unlike with Red Kites and White-Tailed Eagles, these guys weren't given a helping talon. They just came back! A pair of Ospreys, thought to have travelled from Scandinavia, took up residence by Loch Garten, up in the Cairngorms National Park in Scotland. And five years later, in 1959, they bred there, thanks partly to the 24-hour watch the RSPB had going on to make sure they weren't disturbed.

Their numbers only increased very gradually at first thanks to the large-scale use of pesticides like DDT and, amazingly, egg collectors, who were still at it. But by 1980, there were 26 breeding pairs and in 2018, there were 250 pairs. In 1996, a project started which aimed to bring back Ospreys to England and create a self-sustaining population. Osprey chicks were moved from Scotland to Rutland Water, east of Leicester, which was the ideal place because Ospreys had been using it on their migrations to and from Scotland for some time. And in 2001, the first Osprey chick was raised – the first successful breeding in over 160 years in England.

Once they've caught a fish, they bring it around so it's facing head first, which keeps the Osprey as streamlined as possible to reduce wind resistance. And that makes carrying a fish that isn't far off the weight of the Osprey itself that bit easier! They're able to do this because of a number of amazing adaptations. Almost all birds of prey have three forward-facing toes and one facing backwards. But the Osprey has one toe that can rotate forward or backwards. And that means they can have two toes facing forward and two facing backwards, which gives it an extra strong grip and helps it both catch and keep hold of fish. The only other birds of prey with this adaptation are owls. Ospreys also have these barbed pads on the soles of their feet, which help grab something as slippery as a fish. They have valves in their nostrils that completely seal once they hit the water, so water doesn't travel up their nose. They are perfectly suited to catching fish.

Ospreys are summer migrants, travelling to the UK in late spring from Africa, where they'll return in September and October. They're found in every continent in the world except Antarctica (but they aren't that common across Europe, except in Scandinavia). The Peregrine Falcon is the only bird of prey that's more widely distributed around the world. I'm trying to encourage Ospreys to check out my neck of the woods on the west coast of Scotland by making a platform for them. When the chicks become adults, they nest only a few miles away, so if we do attract an Osprey pair, it could be the start of something really special!

SNIPE

Scientific name: *Gallinago gallinago*

Conservation status (UK/Europe): Amber/Least Concern

In three words: Camouflaged, long-billed, shy

Look out for: Skulking through moorland (summer) or marshes (winter) with its small head and long, straight bill; fast zigzagging flight when surprised

How easy it is to see them: Challenging – they blend in so well to the background!

Snipe are incredible creatures. The Great Snipe (*Gallinago media*) can fly without stopping at impressive speeds for over 4,000 miles. A study published in 2021 by Åke Lindström and colleagues revealed that Great Snipes change their altitude around dawn and dusk from approximately 4,000m during the day to 2,000m in the night. Many of them travel at 6,000m, with one recorded flying at 8,700m (Mount Everest is 8,849m, just for context!).

This feat is all thanks to the large stores of fat they put on in autumn before they migrate from their breeding grounds in Scandinavia, northern Europe and Russia to sub-Saharan Africa.

In the UK, we have two species of Snipe – the Common Snipe and the Jack Snipe and they're both really well camouflaged when they're on the ground. The Jack Snipe is smaller, has a shorter bill and flies to the UK for the winter, unlike the Common Snipe, which is a resident here in many parts of the country. But it's their behaviour which really sets them apart. A Jack Snipe's defence mechanism is to completely rely on being camouflaged. It'll crouch down if threatened by something close by, but will only fly away when the intruder is pretty much standing on it. That's the reason they're known as *bécassine soure* in French, which amusingly translates as 'deaf snipe'! When it does fly away, they don't fly very high before dropping back down into cover again.

I especially love when they're wading around looking for food. They bob around like they're bouncing on a pogo stick – or maybe jack-in-the-box is more appropriate. That's not where they get their name though; that's thought to be because 'Jack' has historically referred to something small.

The Common Snipe is quite a bit longer and has a longer bill. They'll flush quicker and call when they do, before flying off quickly and in a bit of a mad panic. But there's method to the madness. After a while, you notice that they're flying in a very particular way – zigzagging across the sky. Males also make this amazing vibrating drumming sound in flight during the spring courtship season. It sounds a bit like a bleat, which is why you hear it nicknamed 'heather bleater' up in Scotland. And that's also what has earned it the name 'taivaanvuohi' in Finland, meaning 'sky goat'. Some people used to think the moorland were haunted, because the noise is so peculiar and it happens during twilight and stops suddenly before reappearing somewhere different. For a long time, the sound was assumed to be a call, but zoologist Philip Manson-Bahr dug a little deeper and discovered that the sound is created by the angle of a Snipe's tail feathers when the bird dives He proved this by sticking two snipe feathers into a cork attached to a long string before spinning it around his head and recreating the sound. He did this in 1931 in front of several members of the British Ornithologists Union at an Italian restaurant in Central London! The longer the dive a Snipe makes, the louder the call is, and that's a signal to the listening female Snipes that this Snipe is the guy to go for. They've also got a distinctive alarm call that sounds like a ticking clock before they take flight, dodging this way and that. They're amazing birds.

TEAL

Name: Teal

Scientific name: *Anas crecca*

Conservation status (UK/Europe): Amber/Least Concern

In three words: Small, colourful, patterned

Look out for: The incredible green eye patches (male); emerald-coloured wing patch

How easy it is to see them: Fairly Easy in winter both by the coast and inland

Ducks are divided up into different families largely depending on how they catch their food. The biggest group by far is the Dabbling Ducks, who feed at the water's surface looking for plant matter like weeds and seeds as well as small invertebrates. Sometimes they'll upend themselves to look for food below the surface but won't dive to catch it. The Mallard is a good example of a Dabbler. Then there are the Diving Ducks, who slip below the surface and swim underwater to catch molluscs, insects and forage for aquatic plants. You will have seen the water slide off their feather like water off . . . you get the picture. You've probably heard of a few Diving Ducks, like the Eider, Goldeneye or Tufted Duck. Lastly, we've got Sawbills, which are Diving Ducks, but they've got unique saw-like, teeth-like projections which help them catch and hold onto fish. There are only six species of Sawbills in the world and four of them you can see around the UK, which is pretty cool.

Overall, there are 22 duck species that you can regularly see in and around the UK (22 if we include two that are somewhere between Ducks and Geese: the Egyptian Goose and the Shelduck). Of the 22, 3 you can only see in the winter (the Smew, although there are only just over a hundred, which come over from Scandinavia and Russia; the Velvet Scoter, which also travel from Russia and Scandinavia, and the Long-tailed Duck, which make the long journey down from the Arctic) and for

15 of the others, they're more numerous in winter than in summer, so get your coat and go see some Ducks. They've come a long way to be here!

I get asked quite a lot about why Ducks seem to look different at different times of the year. The answer is that male Ducks are much more colourful in spring because that's when they're trying to attract a mate, so that's when they need to look their best! After they've been successful with that (or not), the males moult their feathers. That's not that unusual for birds, but the way ducks do it is: they moult their flight feathers all at once. And that's a problem because it means that for around a month, these guys can't actually fly, which makes them especially vulnerable. It also means they can be a lot trickier to identify. Their brightest feathers go first, so males often end up looking much more like the females. So if you see a faded-looking duck in the middle of summer, they're not having a bad hair day, been bleached by the sunlight or anything like that – they're just wearing what we call 'eclipse plumage'. By autumn, they're back to their dapper selves again.

The Teal is a little Dabbling Duck and a pretty one at that, although maybe not the prettiest UK duck. But it depends what you think pretty is, I suppose. The Mandarin is beautiful, but the Teal has got style, with its chestnut head and distinctive, metallic-greenish half-moon shape patch around its eye. The fashionable colour 'teal' is named after this patch, although, to be honest, it doesn't look that similar to the beautiful colour on the bird, which is actually more emerald.

The Teal is actually the smallest of all the ducks that regularly visit or breed in the UK. It's only about two-thirds of the size of a Mallard and only about one-third of the weight. And like the Mallard, males and females look very different (known in the trade as sexual dimorphism). Males have speckled/spotted breasts, grey sides, a long white stripe under their wing that you can see when they're sitting or standing, and a black tail with pale yellow triangular patch to the sides. Everything looks neatly marked and edged, a bit like a jazzy tailored suit. Females are a bit trickier to identify because they're mainly mottled grey-brown and look similar to female Mallards at first glance, although they're a lot smaller. Both male and female have emerald-green patches on their wings, with a similar-sized black patch right next to it, which you can see in flight. And these guys are really impressive fliers. If they're suddenly surprised or frightened, they've got this way of taking off very quickly, almost vertically. That's why the common collective noun for Teal is 'a spring'. Once they're up, they can reach over 50mph and are aerobatic little things, twisting, turning, ducking, diving and swerving this way and that in their pairs or large winter flocks. Sometimes it looks like they're about to land before they wheel away, almost like they suddenly remember that they prefer flying to walking!

Males call out with a kind of piping sound that helps keep the shape of the flock together. They also have a high-pitched whistling call that sounds a bit like 'krik–krik', and that's why the Teal is known as the 'Krickente' in German, 'Krikand' in Danish and 'Kricka' in Swedish.

Only about 2,000 pairs of Teal breed in the UK, mostly in northern parts of the UK in wetlands with nice tall vegetation around. But in winter, up to around 200,000 Teal from Scandinavia and Russia join them, depending on how cold it is over there. If the lakes are frozen, more will head over here to the (relative) warmth of our wetlands, including reservoirs, flooded fields and gravel pits. Their range is incredible in winter – they're found in northern Africa, down through Egypt and Sudan, the Middle East, India, south-east Asia, South Korea and Japan. Pretty impressive.

COASTS

Living by the sea means I have a wide variety of birds on my doorstep. It's actually a little lochan (small loch) with brackish water (freshwater that gets covered with a bit of saltwater now and then), and that means it's such an important place for wildlife. At every time of year there are different bird species in the lochan, which is one of the reasons I love it so much – it's so varied. But there's always the Grey Heron that patrols around and he's got to know me a bit. I think he's probably quite happy to see me when I go and put some food out for the Mallards, Goldeneyes and Red-breasted Mergansers, because some of it gets eaten by the little fish that he'll then hunt for. The lochan is only about 60cm deep, so it's also the perfect place for our local mother otter to teach her pups how to catch fish.

Beyond the lochan is what we just call 'the bay', but it is actually the Sound of Mull – the stretch of water that separates mainland Scotland from the Isle of Mull. And that's where you'll see the last species I've included in the book: the incredible White-tailed Eagle. Save the best till last, eh?! The White Tail is the largest Eagle in Europe and I still can't believe they are only a couple of miles from my doorstep. It still blows my mind every time I see one. It also never ceases to amaze me quite how differently they behave to the other huge bird of prey local to my parts – the Golden Eagle. Goldies are typically a speck in the distance, but you can find yourself feet from a White Tail, especially if you happen to be on a fishing boat!

In this section, you'll find other iconic birds like the Puffin, champion endurance specialist the Arctic Tern and the Chough – a big conservation win. And talking of icons, there's Albie, the only albatross you'll ever likely to see in the northern hemisphere. He spends his time in the Baltic Sea around Germany and Denmark but has decided to spend his summers in the past few years in Northumberland, England. He's attracted quite a fan club!

ARCTIC TERN

Scientific name: *Sterna paradisaea*

Conservation status (UK/Europe): Amber/Secure

In three words: Confident, chatty, protective

Look out for: Black cap, red beak, long, pointy wings with long outer tail feathers; floaty flying style

How easy it is to see them: Fairly Easy on breeding colonies and around the coastline, especially in the summer

I love Terns – they fly so gracefully, almost like tiny little gliders. They're slimmer and more delicate-looking than gulls with thinner, pointier bills, and everything about them is built to fly long distances with as much efficiency as possible. When you see one sitting down or on a post, you will see how long their wings are compared to their bodies, and it looks like they don't have any feet at all. When they're sitting down, their wings stretch so far backwards it looks like a tail – so you might not even realise what you're looking at at first, but it is definitely their wings, folded back and crossed over.

There are five Tern species that breed in the UK: the Arctic Tern, Common Tern, Roseate Tern, Little Tern and Sandwich Tern. You're unlikely to see a Roseate Tern, sadly, because it is the UK's rarest nesting seabird and there are only estimated to be around a hundred breeding pairs left in the UK. Plus, the only regular colony is on Coquet Island off the Northumberland coast. The Arctic Tern is more common around the coasts, but the Common Tern is more common inland, around rivers and reservoirs. The Little Tern nests in a shallow scrape or scoop in a sand or shingle beach just above the tide line, which makes them really vulnerable to disturbance by predators, dogs off leads, etc. Terns have a 'safety in numbers' policy when it comes to nesting, and that's all right if it's a ten-thousand-strong colony. But when you've only got a few dozen of them, a single wandering dog or curious badger can cause serious problems. Thanks to the diligent work of the National Trust, the RSPB and some amazing local volunteers, rangers and wardens, Little Terns have been doing very well in north and east Norfolk in the past couple of years.

And one of those rangers is my friend Chris, who I headed out with a couple of years ago on a site monitoring Sandwich Terns and Little Terns, both of which lay their eggs on sand and shingle beaches not far from the sea. It's not only predators and dogs the rangers have to protect against though, which they do with little fences. There's also a really high tide, which can wash away the whole colony. So, rangers have to keep watch 24/7, and if the tide is about to destroy the whole nesting site, they have to quickly run out, pick up the eggs and place wooden markers into the sand with numbers on them. Then, when the tide's gone back out, all the eggs get put back exactly where they were. Terns also face problems off the ground, too; low-flying aeroplanes send every single member of the Tern colony into the air. So the rangers also work to redirect planes. It's a phenomenal operation, protecting Little Terns and Sandwich Terns, and I've got so much respect for the rangers who work tirelessly to keep these guys safe.

The Arctic Tern is the IronMan/Woman of the bird world. It should really be called the Polar Tern because it doesn't just stay in the Arctic. Many of them travel from the Arctic to the Antarctic and back again every year, meandering their way there and back. That's an average distance of over 44,000 miles, the longest migration by any animal. Some Arctic Terns fly way more than that distance in a year. In 2016, one Arctic Tern, who flew from the Farne Islands of the coast of Northumberland in the UK, down to Antarctica and back, clocked up 59,650 miles, which is well over twice the way around the world. That's an incredible achievement for any animal, but bearing in mind an Arctic Tern weighs a little over 100 grams, has a wingspan of up to 85cm and makes this journey twice a year for the whole of its life (which can be up to 30 years), it does make you feel a bit hopeless when you're out of breath after a ten-minute run. So how on earth do these guys manage it? Well, they eat on the move, dipping down to the ocean surface to eat fish and crustaceans. But that still doesn't quite answer how they can perform this epic feat of endurance. It's truly mind-boggling.

One year, I even followed their migration route because I was asked to do some filming down in Antarctica. I'd been watching an Arctic Tern colony off the coast of the UK with my friend Chris in the summer, and then six months later, I found myself surrounded by Arctic Terns, who'd all flown the 10,000-plus miles down to Antarctica. It was pretty surreal thinking that I might be standing next to the exact same Arctic Terns as I was six months before in the UK, especially when you think about the very different journeys we took to get there!

With their black caps, red bills, long angular wings and pale-grey bodies, they do look very similar to another tern species that visits the UK – the Common Tern. To tell them apart, look for the black tip at the end of the red bill, which identifies the Common Tern and the much longer tail streamers (outer edge tail feathers) of the Arctic Tern, which extend a long way past the other tail feathers. If you want to see Arctic Terns on their breeding grounds, you can find them in Orkney, Shetland and the Farne Islands. But if you're not heading to any of these places, they are summer visitors to the UK coasts before making their way south in early autumn. Some Arctic Terns travel inland during their journey up from the Antarctic in late April and early May, so you can occasionally see them at reservoirs inland as well.

Here's a quick guide to tell the UK Tern species apart, as they do look so similar and are often found in the same place (they've also all got black caps!).

Arctic Tern: Red bill, long tail streamers

Common Tern: Red bill with black tip, short tail streamers

Little Tern: Yellow bill with black tip, short tail, black eyestripe

Roseate Tern (rare): Black bill with reddish base, pinky tinge to breast, long tail streamers

Sandwich Tern: Black bill with yellowish tip, black legs and shaggy black crest. Part of its Latin name, *sandivicensis*, normally refers to a species first found in Hawaii (which used to be known as the South Sandwich Islands) but in this case it refers to the place where the bird was first discovered, which was in Sandwich, Kent.

BLACK-BROWED ALBATROSS

Scientific name: *Thalassarche melanophris*

Conservation status (UK/Europe): N/A

In three words: Gigantic, graceful gliders

Look out for: Huge dark wings; dark shadow above the eyes

How easy it is to see them: There's only one, so head to RSPB Bempton Cliffs from April to see this truly incredible bird

It looks like an artist with a tiny paintbrush coloured in the Black-browed Albatross. And they must have done it on a day that they were at their happiest, sipping a cup of coffee in the sunshine under an umbrella, because they did such a good job. It's actually quite a common bird, but only to the lower reaches of the southern hemisphere. But amazingly, one Black-Browed Albatross, who's been named Albie, has been visiting the UK in recent years, which is utterly incredible! He's become a celebrity, much like John Coe the Orca, who has a really distinctive gouge in his dorsal fin, and hangs around with his best mate Aquarius all over the west coast of the UK.

With Albie, it's a bit of a bittersweet tale, though, because something's not right with his navigational instinct and he can't CTRL-ALT-DEL and start again. So he can't find his way back to his breeding grounds in the South Atlantic. And sadly that means he'll never find a mate, but he seems content to roam the Baltic Sea and make the occasional visit here. He was first spotted at RSPB Bempton Cliffs in the summer of 2017 but wasn't seen again until he returned briefly in June 2020 and June 2021. But 2022 was a really special year because he made a surprise visit in the spring and decided to stay for the whole summer! I want to say a bit about RSPB Bempton Cliffs, because it is a one-of-a-kind reserve on the north Yorkshire coast facing the North Sea. Around

500,000 seabirds come to the 3 miles of huge white chalk cliffs here between March and October to start and raise their families. It's one of the only places you can see Puffins in the UK (among many other species including Gannets and Guillemots).

Albatrosses are among the most amazing creatures on Planet Earth. The Wandering Albatross has the widest wingspan of any bird and can go for years without touching the ground. It actually uses up less energy flying than it does sitting incubating an egg! Albatrosses are more like kites than birds, really, and like Kites, they use the wind to fly. They've learned to rise up at an angle from the trough of a wave. As the bird travels higher, the wind gets faster, so they gain airspeed, climbing around 10–15 metres above the ocean before banking downwind towards another wave trough. It's a corkscrew-like pattern known as dynamic soaring, and means they don't even need to flap their wings to travel thousands of miles. It's like they're travelling on a cushion of air that helps them ride the waves. Wandering Albatrosses use this technique to circumnavigate the globe, which they can do in just 46 days. They even sleep in flight, taking power naps that can just last a few seconds. And I've seen their synchronised courtship display rituals up close when I was shooting a film out in the South Sandwich Islands, on an island named, appropriately, Bird Island, and they wouldn't be out of place on *Strictly*, they're that impressive. I felt like I was living in a fairy tale. But that wasn't the thing that impressed me most.

Some Albatrosses even create their own runway – a long, thin strip of grass kept short by the amount it gets trampled on by the birds – which is situated close to their nests. The runway faces the oncoming wind and even comes complete with both an area to taxi before they build up the speed to take off and paths leading to their nests, which are a bit like terminals! The reason why the strip faced the oncoming wind is exactly why runways in the UK tend to be east–west, because the wind comes from the west and you want to fly into the wind on take-off to maximise the amount of lift you get. Just imagine running into the wind and you'll get that feeling that you could take off if this was a bit stronger.

Everyone should get the chance to see an Albatross at least once it their lifetime. And, while we're talking about how amazing Albatrosses are, I've got to mention Wisdom. Sometimes kids ask me how old birds live for. Well, Wisdom is one bird that's breaking all sorts of records. She's a wild Laysan Albatross (Laysan is the name of the breeding colony in the north-western islands of Hawaii) and she is thought to have hatched in 1951. She was tagged by a scientist at the Midway Atoll National Wildlife Refuge (Midway forms part of the Hawaiian Islands) in 1956 after she laid an egg, so she was estimated to be about 5 years old, the age at which they're able to breed. She's now 71 years old (as at 2022) and the United States Geological Survey reckon she's covered over 3,000,000 miles in her lifetime. Just to put that into perspective, that's the equivalent of travelling all the way around the world 120 times. She has a long-term mate, called Akeakamai (which quite beautifully translates as 'lover of wisdom' in the Hawaiian language) and the last chick they reared was, incredibly, in 2020. She's had at least 30 chicks in her lifetime! Akeakamai usually arrives at the nesting site a couple of days before Wisdom (they spend the rest of the year roaming the ocean independently), and then they'll perform their complicated courtship dance when they see each other again before mating. It's an incredible thing to see. But, sadly, Akeakamai didn't return in the breeding season of either 2021 or 2022 so let's hope for better news in 2023.

Wisdom's story is a remarkable one, but the Laysan Albatrosses nesting on Midway Atoll are plagued by tonnes of plastic that get dumped into the ocean and end up there. Because of the way the Laysan Albatross catches its food – by skimming the ocean's surface with its beak – they can accidentally pick up plastic, which they then feed to their chicks. It's estimated that 5 tonnes of plastic gets accidentally fed to Laysan Albatross chicks at this breeding site each year. And the chicks can't regurgitate it so it ends up filling up their stomachs, which can cause all sorts of problems for their long-term health and ability to reproduce.

CHOUGH

Scientific name: *Pyrrhocorax pyrrhocorax*

Conservation status (UK/Europe): Green/Secure

In three words: Inquisitive, acrobatic, family-orientated

Listen/look out for: 'Chaarrrrrr!' call; a crow with red feet and a long, red, curved beak in the agricultural field next to the coast

How easy it is to see them: Hard – only in Cornwall, south and west Wales in the UK; still widespread in Spain, though

The Chough (pronounced 'chuff' in case you're wondering, because the English language can go either way!) is the rarest member of the crow family (Corvids) to breed in Britain. South Stack, which is a tiny island connected to Holy Island in Anglesey, at the north-west tip of Wales, is one of the best places to see them. The RSPB have got a reserve there facing South Stack island and the first time I went there, I remember hearing a loud 'Chaarrrrrrrr', and thinking, *I've never heard that sound before.* Then, lo and behold, I see red legs, and a red beak and I knew that it was a Chough. They were on their way to the nearby fields to probe cow poo for little insects and worms. So, if you want to find a Chough, I'd check and see which field the livestock have just moved from and wait near the cowpats!

Cornwall is very proud of the Chough, so much so, that it's standing proudly above the shield on the county's coat of arms. According to Cornish legend, when King Arthur died, his soul transformed into a Chough. The bright red beak and feet supposedly represents his violent end at the hands of Mordred. Sadly, though, as a result of long-term habitat loss (the livestock that used to graze the areas around cliffs, where the Chough would eat insects and insect larvae, were moved inland), persecution and egg collecting, Chough numbers were in decline since at least the end of the 18th century. The last breeding happened in 1947 and the last Chough, who had been living near Newquay, died in 1973. Apart from the odd fleeting sighting, that was thought to be that.

And then, unexpectedly, in 2001, a small group (or 'chatter') of wild Choughs appeared on the Lizard peninsula in south Cornwall and decided to stay. Two of the group of five birds became a pair, and the next year, they nested and produced three young Choughs. Hallelujah! The first wild Choughs in Cornwall for over 50 years. After this historic event, the RSPB, English Nature (now called Natural England) and the National Trust got together to form the Cornish Chough Project. The nesting site was monitored 24 hours a day by RSPB staff and local volunteers, to protect it from disturbance. The plan worked, and over the next 11 years, this amazing pair raised 46 chicks. They both passed away in 2013, but their legacy remains, and the range of the Chough is continuing to grow through Cornwall! Meanwhile, the Cornish Chough Project has become The Cornish Chough Conservation Network. They keep monitoring nesting sites in spring and encourage local farmers to graze their livestock near the cliffs, not use fertiliser on fields near to the cliffs and go for alternative worming treatments on their cattle, which don't make their cowpats sterile. This all helps give the Choughs the best chance to thrive. Thankfully, the Chough is still quite widespread in Spain but in other parts of Europe its numbers are quite small, in isolated areas of France, Italy, Portugal and Greece.

EIDER

Scientific name: *Somateria mollissima*
Conservation status (UK/Europe): Amber/Endangered
In three words: Chunky, fast, powerful
Look out for: A large white-and-black duck with a big,
wedge-shaped bill, greenish neck and pinky breast
(male); barred grey-brown colour (female); look for
fast, low-flying flocks
How easy it is to see them: Challenging – look in
winter around the coasts but more common north of
Northumberland and along Scandinavian coasts

The Eider is a truly incredible duck for lots of different reasons. Everything about it is impressive. First, it's the largest duck to grace our shores in the UK, weighing in at up to 2.8kg. It's also our fastest, capable of flying over 60mph. I call them 'flying pecs' because when you look at them, they're basically just one big chest muscle! And that's what makes them such powerful flyers.

It also has the warmest feathers in the animal kingdom, which can keep it alive in the sub-zero temperatures of the Arctic. The Eider is a serious diving Duck. It doesn't mess about in ponds. It's a proper sea duck and can dive up to around 20 metres, searching the seabed for molluscs, especially mussels, but also urchins and crabs. They do love mussel farms, where the mussels are attached to a long rope, because the Eiders aren't having to dive around into the sediment on the sea floor. It's a bit like fast-food to an Eider, but it doesn't make them massively popular with mussel farmers. It swallows mussels whole, using its gizzard (the hind part of the stomach, which has thick muscular walls and a rough, horned lining) to crush them up. It even does the same with urchins, spines and all! With all these rich pickings, an Eider can eat its own bodyweight in a single day.

Its scientific name, *Somateria mollissima*, translates from Latin as 'softest down body', and that's because their down feathers (the very soft ones next to the duck's skin, mainly around the chest) are the warmest of any creature in the world. That's why a particularly expensive type of duvet is called an eiderdown – because it's made from the down feathers of an Eider Duck. Thankfully, this now doesn't involve killing these amazing birds – the down can be harvested after the ducklings leave the nest, so no one gets hurt.

Males and females look very different, like Mallards, but both have distinctively sloped heads with long, wedge-shaped bills that extend right up next to their eyes. Male Eiders are quite spectacular-looking, with their black-and-white pattern, delicate pale-green patches on the back of their necks and a beautiful rosy tinge to their breasts. But my favourite thing about the male is their call, which they use when they're displaying. They throw their heads back and make a kind of 'oooooooohhhh' noise, which sounds a lot like an old lady being surprised by something, if you can imagine that! Females are mottled brown, but that varies from grey-brown to red-brown. Darker than a female Mallard, basically. Still beautiful, but less flashy than the males. The females deserve a special mention here, though, because they pull out an incredible feat of endurance. They make sure their eggs hatch at all costs, so they sit on them for around 26 days. They won't be scared away by anything. They'll only ever leave to drink once every few days and when they do, they leave a bit of down on top of the eggs so it just looks like a fluff ball. They don't eat a thing the whole time. That's commitment.

You sometimes hear Eider Ducks nicknamed 'Cuddy Ducks', especially in Northumberland, and that comes from a connection with St Cuthbert (c.634–687), the monk, hermit and later Bishop of Lindisfarne. That's the tidal island off the coast of Northumberland also known as Holy Island that you can get to in the car, but need to keep one eye on your watch or you'll find yourself facing a completely submerged road at high tide. The legend goes that Cuthbert moved to Lindisfarne, aged about 30, and ran the monastery there. He became fascinated with seabirds and discovered that local people were eating the Eider Ducks, other seabirds and their eggs that they found on Lindisfarne and the Farne Islands, a few miles to the south-east. He is said to have introduced laws to make it illegal to eat the ducks or the eggs. It's believed that this was the first official bird protection legislation in history, over 1300 years before the Sea Birds Preservation Act of 1869, which the UK government introduced to protect birds of prey and seabirds during their breeding season. See, it was worth the diversion talking about an old guy called Cuthbert!

The great news is that Northumberland is still associated with Eider Ducks, where they live year-round. You can also find them along much of the

Scottish coast and Cumbria, and in winter, much of the rest of the coast of England. You'll never see them flying high up – they'll always be 5 metres up or less. But their numbers are falling, particularly in Iceland, Finland, Norway and Greenland (and together, they account for nearly three-quarters of all Eiders in Europe). In fact, their numbers have fallen so much (and are projected to keep doing so) that the Eider has been moved into the 'Endangered' category on the 2021 European Red List of Birds, the review of all 544 species of birds that occur regularly in Europe.

HERRING GULL

Scientific name: *Larus argentatus*
Conservation status (UK/Europe): Red/Threatened
In three words: Opportunistic, intelligent bruiser
Look out for: Your chips! These fearless seaside birds
are hard to miss but look out for the little circle on the
lower part of the jaw
How easy it is to see them: Really Easy

When I was a kid, I said the word 'seagull' in front of a bunch of old birders and I saw them looking at each other and smirking. One of them piped up with something like: 'Er, actually, there's no such thing as a seagull. It's a common misconception. There are several species of gull native to the UK but the most common and the one I think you're referring to is the Herring Gull.' I think he meant well, but it did come off a bit smug, like he was 'birdsplaining'. I try to do things a bit differently because I think people switch off when they feel they're being talked down to. What I tend to say to someone who seems interested is, 'Can you tell me something about a seagull?' And that usually invites a funny response. 'They steal your chips!', 'One ate my ice cream and left me with just half a cone!', 'One flew off with my nan's Chihuahua!', and I love that. Sometimes, the person or someone in the group I'm talking to will know the Herring Gull fact, and I love that too, because they've already taken enough of an interest in birds to remember it. And if no one knows it, well, you can swoop in with the Herring Gull fact or one of the other amazing things about them!

So, it's true – there's no such thing as a 'seagull'. There are over a hundred species of Gull around the world (some of which are found a long way away from the sea) and six of them we can regularly see in the UK. The one that will sometimes nick your chips if you're facing the other way on Brighton beach is the Herring Gull.

Although they seem like they're common when you're by the seaside, they're actually now one of the 70 species on the UK Red List.

They're one of those species, like Pigeons, that really divide people. I get it. But one way of looking at them is that they're resourceful and adaptable birds that have just found a way to live in a tough world! They do get a bad rep for being a bit thick, partly thanks to their amusing appearance in *Finding Nemo* where they only say, 'Mine!' But these guys are pretty smart. If you've ever seen a Herring Gull on a patch of grass running on the spot and wondered what on earth it's doing, you're not the only one! They've learned that the pitter-patter of rain makes earthworms come to the surface. So they stamp their feet to mimic rainfall and then gobble up the gullible worms. That's pretty impressive. They've also learned to drop anything with a shell onto a hard surface from a height to crack it. They're also pretty amazing parents. Male and female Herring Gulls co-parent, each spending time incubating eggs, both feeding their chicks and putting up with 24-hour demands for food even after they've just had a full meal! If you look closely at an adult Herring Gull's beak, you'll see a blood-red spot on the lower mandible. It's actually a visual cue for the chick to use, tapping on the red spot so that the mum regurgitates food for it. But it's more than this – the red spot is like a button that operates a machine, so the Herring Gull will *only* regurgitate food if the chick presses the button.

Plus, unlike us, Herring Gulls can actually drink sea water, because they've got these special glands connected to their bills that filter out the salt. And if you're still not sold, they help to keep rats away because anything edible that hits the floor they'll have long before a rat can get to it! Oh, and if you are keen to enjoy your fish and chips on the beach, the best way to deter a Herring Gull is to look it in the eye. They're much more likely to go for someone looking the other way!

NORTHERN GANNET

Scientific name: *Morus bassanus*

Conservation status (UK/Europe): Amber/Secure

In three words: Big, powerful plunge-diver

Look out for (in flight): A large, streamlined white glider with black wingtips; distinctive pointed head and long beak

How easy it is to see them: Fairly Easy – around coasts in the UK, Ireland and Western Europe; massive breeding colonies

The Northern Gannet is the UK's largest seabird and they're pretty distinctive birds with their long necks, white pointy beaks with thick dark grooves and edges, pale-yellow heads and bright white plumage which extends to the half of the wing nearest its body; the other half of the wing (the primary feathers and wingtips) are black.

You can see them offshore all around the UK, but the best place to find them on the mainland is at RSPB Bempton Cliffs on the east Yorkshire coast and at RSPB Troup Head, about 45 miles north of Aberdeen. They nest in large colonies (called gannetries) but I've always found their decision-making process quite funny. Sometimes they'll be a perfectly good-looking rock 30 metres away, but instead of splitting their numbers so they'll have more space, they're happier all crammed in together. Maybe it's a safety in numbers mentality. The biggest Gannet colony in the world is Bass Rock, a 107-metre-high volcanic rock over a mile offshore in the Firth of Forth, just 30 miles east of Edinburgh. In peak breeding season, it houses around 150,000 Gannets and they have 'Gannet Cams' set up so you can watch them live. The noise is just incredible! The smell is also incredible, but for different reasons (!). They start arriving at the end of February and stay until late October when they head towards the Mediterranean and the north-west coast of Africa for winter.

Their long, pointed wings, which can reach up to 2 metres across, are designed for gliding low over the water while they're looking for fish, but they're not great for smooth take-offs and landings. That's one of the reasons they like remote sea cliffs to nest on, which also provide strong updraughts of wind, which help them take off. But it's the behaviour more than their description than makes Gannets unmistakable. Watching these incredible birds dive into the water in large groups to catch fish is something special. They plunge into the sea at heights of about 30 metres, folding their wings in just before they reach the surface, which they hit at 60mph. I've seen them all diving together near the Ardnamurchan Lighthouse not far from me, and they look like little black-and-white missiles raining down on the water, with little white splashes shooting back up to the surface, like tiny Olympic divers off the high dive. It's incredible to watch, to the extent that a couple of times, I've actually forgotten to turn my camera on to film them. But how can they keep doing this without breaking their necks? Well, their heads come complete with airbags! They have a complex arrangement of tiny air cushions under the skin to help absorb the force. They've also got one of the strongest necks of any bird, and those two features together help to stop it from getting concussed, which is what would happen if any other creature tried to do what these guys can do! They also have to get the timing right, as well as the angle, too. They need to allow for refraction in the water, because where you think the fish might be when you're above the water isn't where the fish actually are below the surface. They've got to calculate this at the same time, so there's a lot more than you might think going through a Gannet's head before it hits the water. Sometimes, if they're not happy about something, they'll bail out of their dive really late on, and it looks like a fighter jet pulling a high G-force climb.

PUFFIN

Scientific name: *Fratercula arctica*

Conservation status (UK/Europe): Red/Secure

In three words: Colourful, charismatic, small

Look out for: A little black-and-white coastal bird with a large, orangey triangular beak; in flight, they beat their wings very fast and their beaks look rounded

How easy it is to see them: Fairly Easy – in early spring/ summer, they'll be at their large breeding colonies in Wales, Scotland, northern England, Northern Ireland, the Republic of Ireland, off the coast of Brittany and along the Norwegian coast

Who doesn't love Puffins? With their multi-coloured bills, cartoonish faces and waddling walk, it's no wonder these guys get affectionately nicknamed 'Clowns of the sea' or 'Sea Parrots'. There are two things that always surprise people about Puffins: they're only about the size of a Diet Coke can, and the UK is actually one of the best places in the world to see them. We've got over half a million of them breeding, although half of them are found at a handful of sites. But if you know where to go, you'll be rewarded!

I went to see them on Lunga Island. It's one of the best places to see them in the UK and it's only a 20-mile ferry trip from where I live. I went there to film Puffins for just over a month, although the sea was so rough that I ended up stuck on the island! I had to text my Scottish father, Chris, to ask him to come and rescue me in his RIB, although the sea was still so rough, I wasn't sure when he'd actually be able to cross. I hadn't seen another person in a long time and I was losing it a bit, to the point that I started filming myself singing 'I Will Survive' in a very high-pitched voice. Meanwhile, Chris was filming his attempted rescue trip and the first I saw Chris was actually through my camera. When I did, I frantically packed up all my stuff and ran over to where he was heroically holding onto a rock. So although I had a magical few weeks with the Puffins (and Manx Shearwaters and Storm Petrels) I was so happy to be homebound!

At the beginning of August, the parents leave their burrow with the Pufflings (that is the name of a baby Puffin, yes!) inside but only a few days before they're ready to fledge. Then it's down to the pufflings to choose a night to leave on, and then they all fly away. I wonder what they're all chatting about and how they decide the moment's right. They have the instinct to head out to the Atlantic and their feet won't touch the ground for five years after that, which is incredible. If they could incubate their eggs on water, they would never need to come to land, but that's the only reason they return.

When they're on the land, they're vulnerable, which is why they create burrows for their nests using their beaks and feet. These burrows are completely dark inside, so you wonder how the chick deals with that. Well, the orange on the adult Puffins beaks are bioluminescent, and being out in the sun effectively 'charges' them. The pufflings can see the beak in the burrow and are guided towards it.

Their wings aren't perfectly designed for flying – like Penguins', they're meant to work as paddles or rudders to propel them through the water, and they can dive up to around 60 metres for fish, especially sand eels, small, long eel-like fish. You can kind of tell that Puffins aren't that comfortable flying because they've got these short, stubby wings and it looks like it takes a lot of effort to fly. Still, they can reach an impressive 55mph, beating their wings up to 400 times a minute to achieve that kind of speed.

The Latin name for Puffin is *Fratercula arctica*, which means 'little brother of the north', one of the more beautiful scientific names! It's thought to refer to the fact their black-and-white plumage is similar to the robes of a friar. Aside from the striking black-and-white plumage, the first thing you usually notice about a Puffin is its incredible triangular beak that is almost as large as its entire face. Its bright, multi-coloured, but mostly orange beak almost looks like it's been painted on; it's so vivid and well defined. They actually lose the bright orange colour in winter, both on the beaks and feet, and their faces go from bright white to dark grey. The fact that their beaks become so bright in summer is because the fish they eat contain a pigment called carotenoid, and it's thought that females react to a brighter beak in the male because it indicates a stronger potential mate.

You often see photographs of Puffins carrying several little fish in their beaks. They're able to hold the fish they catch underwater thanks to their strong, ridged tongue, hinged jawbones and serrations on the inside of their specialised beaks. That's how they usually emerge from the water with around ten fish all neatly lined up. Unlike many other birds, they don't regurgitate food for their young – the fish come straight back in the Puffin's beak and get transferred to the Puffling. Parents take it in turns to do the fishing duty and incubating the one egg that the female lays. And they'll usually return to the same burrow each year. If you don't fancy making the trip to see them, there are a couple of popular 'PuffinCams' that volunteers have set up in the Shetland Isles, Coquet Island in Northumberland and Alderney.

STONECHAT

Scientific name: *Saxicola rubicola*
Conservation status (UK/Europe): Green/Not Evaluated
In three words: Confident, visible, sentry-like
Look out for: A Robin-sized dark-hooded bird with orange breast sitting on a gorse stem or on a rock
How easy it is to see them: Fairly Easy near coasts and on open heaths

The Stonechat is a bird that might surprise some people. If you live in a city, you'll be familiar with garden birds like Blue Tits, Great Tits, Robins and maybe a Great Spotted Woodpecker, but you've probably never heard of a Stonechat! They're about the size of a Robin, and males have a similar orange-red breast, which contrasts strikingly with their black head and white stripe on the side of their neck. Female Stonechats and juveniles are also gorgeous birds, just a bit of a paler brown than the male with black streaks on their heads and backs and with a slightly paler orange breast.

You understand why they're called Stonechats when you hear their call, which sounds exactly like the noise you get when you tap two stones together. They do like hanging out on rocks (the first part of their Latin name, *Saxicola*, means 'rock dweller'), in scrubby land on the top of small shrubs, on fence posts, and anywhere with heather or gorse bushes. Stonechats are common around coasts but also in moorlands, heathland, hills and mountains and they won't be afraid to sit in full view on top of a rock or the highest part of a small shrub.

Stonechats also never seem to look relaxed! They're always moving their tail up and down or flicking their wings, dropping down to investigate something then flitting straight back up to another one of their favourite perches. This alertness might be the reason that Stonechats have been filmed being followed around by the equally beautiful Dartford Warbler (see page 141) in heathland in southern England, taking the opportunity to catch insects near and under their companion. The Stonechat doesn't seem to do that well out of the friendship, though, because it doesn't catch as much when the Warbler's around. But, it does mean that you might see two of the amazing birds featured in this book for the price of one, especially if you're off to the south coast of England for your holidays! Or in hilly, coastal parts of southern Europe with a nice, fast-flowing stream, for that matter.

WHITE-TAILED EAGLE

Scientific name: *Haliaeetus albicilla*

Conservation status (UK/Europe): Amber/Secure

In five words: Magnificent, massive, conservation success story

Look out for: Distinctive white tail (adult); huge brown wings with paler neck and head

How easy it is to see them: Hard – vast majority near west coast of Scotland, but range expanding with reintroduction programmes; also found across north-eastern Europe and parts of Scandinavia

I'm lucky enough to have White-tailed Eagles, also called Sea Eagles, just across the bay from me, and I can't tell you how much I love that. I love all eagles to be honest.

The White-tailed Eagle is another conservation success story. They're the largest birds of prey in the UK (and Europe), and actually the fourth largest bird of prey in the world, with adults measuring up to around 90cm with wingspans that can stretch around 2.5m – the longest of any Eagle in the world. But, like with Red Kites, they were hunted to extinction and by 1918, the last wild White-tailed Eagle in the UK had been shot and killed.

Roy Dennis, an amazing naturalist and expert in reintroducing species that have been lost from habitats, released young White-tailed Eagles on Fair Isle (roughly halfway between the Orkneys and the Shetlands) in 1968, and while it didn't succeed as hoped it did lay the groundwork for future projects. In 1975, the RSPB and NCC re-introduced them on the Isle of Rum in the Inner Hebrides. A total of 75 White-tailed Eagle young were reintroduced between 1975 and 1985. The Eaglets were brought over from Norway (which has a stable population of White Tails), from eagle nests that had two or three chicks in them (they'd take one for the relocation project, which isn't a cruel thing to do – it gives the remaining chick or chicks a higher chance of survival as the parents have one fewer mouth to feed). And 1985 was a happy year because the first eaglets born from reintroduced White Tails appeared. Over the next few years, the population grew slowly though, so another 56 young White Tails were reintroduced between 1993 and 1998. The latest reintroduction project has been in the Isle of Wight in 2019, which was fitting because the last place in the south of England that a breeding pair of White Tails had been seen was Culver Cliff on the east coast of the island in 1780. The project is a collaboration between Forestry England and the Roy Dennis Wildlife Foundation and has used single chicks (again from a brood of two or three) but this time from the population of White Tails in western Scotland, which is great news. And in 2024 (it takes White Tails around five years to reach breeding age), we might hear some even greater news.

There are now around 150 breeding pairs of White Tails in Scotland, 22 of which are on the Isle of Mull. There are about the same number of Golden Eagles as well, which is why Mull is now sometimes referred to as Eagle Island. But the reintroduction of the White Tails has had a big boost to the island's economy, with more and more people wanting to see them. An RSPB study from March 2022 estimated that between £4.9 million and £8 million of tourist money is coming into Mull because of the White Tails.

One of the breeding pairs of White Tails has picked a spot just across from my house to live in, and I feel so lucky that I get to live so close to them. From the first day I became a wildlife cameraman, I've wanted to film an Eagle in its nest. The only trouble is, White-tailed Eagles tend to choose the tops of really tall trees to build their nests in. But I got lucky, because the tree they went for I could see into from a hide I built on a hillside. Although, to be fair, that was a good 90-minute hike away, carrying around 40kg of camera and equipment. But it was so worth it because in 2019, two chicks were born and I made it my mission to film every second from the time they hatched to the time they fledged. And when you're there, there's no feeling like it. You're the only human around who gets to see inside an Eagle's nest, see the chicks being fed, see who's fighting with whom today, whether a big sister is annoying her brother or vice versa. It's mind-boggling to me.

The White-tailed Eagle is more of a vulture than an eagle, really. Compared to the Golden Eagle, which will happily hunt all day, every day and does occasionally come down to scavenge, the White-tailed Eagle is the exact opposite. It'll spend almost all of its time scavenging, and if it hasn't been having much luck and is getting hungry, it'll go out and hunt live prey. Golden Eagles are quite shy and want to hide away from you as much as possible but the White-tailed Eagle will fly over your head and have a good look at you. The White Tail will happily come down and swipe fish that have just been chucked off the side of boats in full view of 20 people in broad daylight standing on the deck of the boat. They're not fussy and they'll even put on a show. So while they're both eagles, they act completely differently.

I've seen White Tails follow Gannets, wait for them to dive for mackerel, successfully grab one and glide back to the surface, before they're greeted by a huge White-tailed Eagle trying to nick it off them. The other thing I've seen them go for is wrasse, a fish that is used to eat the lice off the salmon in the salmon farms nearby. Otters can catch the wrasse that don't dive too deep but otters are messy eaters and will often leave big chunks that the White Tails will hoover up. They've acquired the nickname 'barn doors' because they are that big, but I prefer 'flying kites'.

I've nicknamed the local pair of White-tailed Eagles who live just across the bay Agatha and Lawrence. I named them that because White-tailed Eagles behave a bit like two old people who are happy with each other's company, sitting in comfy chairs, doing the crossword or reading the newspaper and heading out for a wee stroll in the early afternoon when it's not raining. They might stop off at a tea room or a pub for a well-priced soup of the day and roll. That is genuinely not far off the life of a White-tailed Eagle.

A FEW FINAL THOUGHTS

One of the things I love most about birding is seeing other people get the bug for it. I remember how exciting it was when I was a kid, sitting and waiting and being rewarded by catching sight of birds I'd never seen or heard before. One thing that really helped inspire me was seeing how passionate, engaging and friendly fellow birders were. I looked about as different as was possible compared with the people in the first RSPB hide my mum dropped me off at, but it made no difference. The only thing that anyone there really cared about was seeing birds and chatting about them with other people who shared their passion. I was so enthusiastic and keen to learn that I quickly became part of the club.

When I got into twitching, which involves birders travelling sometimes serious distances to see a particular bird – often a rare or unusual one that's turned up somewhere unexpectedly – I found there was a big social side to it. That's partly because it makes sense for birders to travel together, and when you're spending ten hours in the car with four other people, some of whom you've never met before, you get to know them pretty quickly! I remember really fondly going on long drives all over the country – to Scotland, Brighton, Norfolk, Cornwall, and we'd be chipping money in for petrol, sharing the driving duties, taking it in turns to be in charge of the music and keeping the driver awake. Everyone would be helping in some way. And we'd be chattering about birds for much of the way.

After we'd seen the bird or birds, we always head out for a cup of tea, a chat and a bite to eat somewhere. It's the same when you head out locally with birders in late spring to listen to the dawn chorus, when the birds begin to sing at the start of a new day. It's an incredible experience, like hearing each member of an orchestra turn up and start playing until suddenly, you've got a symphony going on. And seeing as you've probably been up since 4am, by 10am, you're absolutely starving! So you end up sitting and chatting about the incredible experience you just shared together over some grub. I've found that with anyone who shares the same passion as you, you will never not have something to talk about. Sometimes I'd be chatting until dawn the next day!

Family birding trips are a different animal to the twitching adventures I went on, but they can be even more magical. Seeing the wonder in a kid's eyes when they identify a bird without your help makes me a very happy man. Something I always do and encourage others to do is to try and imagine the world through a child's eyes. If I see a feather, I'll pick it up, examine it, ask the kids which bird they think it might have come from, how it might have come off the bird and what they think happens to the old feathers and if new feathers appear. It's a great way of getting them to think and imagine.

One great event to get people of all ages looking for birds is the RSPB's 'Big Garden Birdwatch'. It's a fun annual event in the last weekend of January that anyone can take part in. It started in 1979 as a kids' activity for the Young Ornithologists' Club (the YOC) and 34,000 kids took part. From 2001 it's been open to everyone and in 2021, over a million people joined in, which is just phenomenal. The 'Big Garden Birdwatch' is a citizen science project, where all you need to do is sit down in your garden or look out over a garden if you're in a flat, make yourself a cup of tea and count the number of bird species you see in an hour. Believe it or not, the first time I took part was actually 2022. It's such a useful project for charting the number of bird species around the country and engaging people in the natural world. I'm lucky enough to have a garden. It's not a massive space – maybe 4 metres by 3 metres – and I deliberately don't cut the grass because I want it to be as wild as possible. I want the seeds to drop and germinate and turn into lovely wildflowers, which attract all the birds that I love.

If you don't have binoculars and you want to get kids involved, save up the cardboard cylinders from the inside of two toilet rolls, Sellotape them together and you've got a fun pair of your own. That's what I did as a kid before I got my first proper pair! Once the kids see a bird, tell them what it is and before you know it, they'll be telling you what's in the garden before you can even see a bird!

Sadly, the 'Big Garden Birdwatch' tells us that so many birds are declining in numbers, some really dramatically. But if we want to change things, we have to get people interested and involved. I really do believe that if you give kids the chance to fall in love with Mother Nature they will make this world a better place.

Back in January 2022, I interviewed the actor Sam West and we talked all about the 'Big Garden Birdwatch'. He was counting the number of bird species in his garden with his four-year-old daughter, and he mentioned the call of the Wood Pigeon sounding like 'I'm not your pigeon'. I love the idea that they're singing that and it reminded me of the call of the Yellowhammer, which sounds like 'Little bit of bread, no cheese'. It's a great way to remember bird songs. The Great Tit has a song that sounds like 'Tea-cher, Teacher'. Some birds, like the Cuckoo and the Chiffchaff are named for the calls they make, so they're easy to remember. But it's fun to make up your own versions to remember them – I always love hearing what people come up with. For me, one of my favourite bird calls that I can hear from my garden is the Oystercatcher, which sounds like 'Beady, Beady, Beady', so I often just call them 'Beadies'.

When people are interested, I might try and give them some facts about how this bird has been thriving, or this one needs a little help. I try to go about with a gentle, upbeat, reminding voice that informs and inspires people, conveying messages like: when you're sweeping or hoovering up the leaves in autumn, think about leaving a few out there on the ground because solitary bees use them for insulation in the winter. It's that kind of thing I want people to remember when they're mowing the lawn. Because we need our bees. According to the WWF, around 90 per cent of wild plants and three-quarters of global crops rely on animal pollinators. And the honey bee is the most important pollinator around. Lighting that spark in people is so important, and once the fire is going, you can always keep adding to it.

I've carried a slightly child-like sense of wonder with me throughout my life. I'm not sure why I have it, but I'm so glad I do. I don't want to grow up and forget all the fun stuff like being outside exploring and getting my fingernails dirty. We're missing a bit of that today, with kids spending so much time on their phones, so I try to encourage getting out and about whenever I can. If I can get someone interested in birds, that can become a really powerful force in them. Give Mother Nature a bit of space and they're going to love it.

But at school, kids are often learning facts by rote, being told to sit still and don't mess about. Sometimes I feel like we're not teaching them to use their imaginations enough until you're in an English class and your teacher's asking you to use your imagination to write a beautiful story. When that happened to me at school, I kept thinking, *but you've been telling us so often not to use our imaginations*?! I just wish we had a more creative, tailored form of education where we're not just hunting grades, but we're growing as people.

I think it would be amazing to introduce a school subject like environmental science or even ecotourism that encourages young people to pursue a career supporting nature. I'm a big supporter of apprenticeships, especially for people who have developed a passion for something early on. They're one of the best things because you're getting paid for it and you're learning from someone who's usually been in that line of work for decades. In a way, as an apprentice, you're fast-tracking your career because you will have spent four years learning skills in something you're passionate about instead of four years in university racking up a big debt. So many of my friends went to university, studied for a degree in something and ended up doing something completely different. There's nothing wrong with working out what you want to do later in life, but it would be amazing if we could harness young people's passion and help them pursue that as a career. I followed my dream and was lucky enough to get the support I needed from my family and my teachers. That's what set me on the path to where I am now. The courage, persistence, self-sufficiency and the fair amount of stubbornness you need to become a wildlife camera operator I've picked up myself!

I especially love inspiring people who haven't had the opportunity to experience nature as a consequence of disadvantage. There are some visible and invisible barriers that do get in the way for people of colour, both to easily access nature and to find a job in the environmental sector. At the moment, only 0.6 per cent of people in the environmental sector are people of colour (according to a 2017 study from think-tank Policy Exchange). I wish there were more people from ethnic backgrounds working in conservation but there are a few reasons why there aren't at the moment. People around my age might be the second- or third-generation immigrants to the UK. The first two generations were typically low-earning grafters, coming here from overseas and making ends meet for their families by running a shop, driving a taxi, working as a hospital orderly, that sort of thing. It's only my generation that can even contemplate a job in something like conservation, and sometimes they'll be coming up against parents who want something steadier and more stable as a career choice. And that's probably just motivated by not wanting to see their children struggle, as they did. It doesn't mean that Black people aren't interested in wildlife – nothing could be further from the truth.

Part of the problem is that only 3.2 per cent of the rural population (according to the government's 'Population Statistics for Rural England', published in March 2023) are from minority ethnic groups, so many people will need to travel further to reach green spaces, which means they need to spend more time and money. That is sometimes time and money that they don't have. There's also the issue that voluntary work is often a gateway into full-time paid work, which is possible for those with families who can help them out financially, but for those coming from lower-income families, this kind of career choice might not be possible. My role models were both white men – David Attenborough and Steve Irwin – and I love them dearly, but in order to inspire people from all sorts of different backgrounds, it does help if people who look like you and sound like you are represented on television, radio and podcasts.

It's happening, but slowly, with incredible people like Dr Mya-Rose Craig (aka Birdgirl), David Lindo (aka The Urban Birder) and organizations like Flock Together (set up by Ollie Olanipekun and Nadeem Perera) and Girls Who Click, which brings together women nature photographers. Thanks to people like this, the birding community is bigger and more diverse than it's ever been.

Everyone should get the opportunity to get out and do what they love. And who knows, maybe your passion might become a career at some point in your life. I was really lucky that my parents wanted me to follow my dreams. I want to repay their faith in me by doing something important with my work. I want to help the next generation to become even better conservationists, biologists, cameramen and women. And I want to inspire people to go about life with a smile on their face. It's a beautiful world, after all, but we're damaging it quicker than we can repair it. We need to do more to save it. And we can!

THANK YOU

First of all, I'd like to thank both sets of parents – my parents Ahmed and Ilham, and my Scottish parents Chris and Amanda.

Thanks to my brother Karrar and his wife Roberta for being so supportive of me throughout my early career.

I would like to thank my school – Wellingborough – for the help and diagnosis of my dyslexia. I'd also like to thank Bangor University for teaching me and opening my eyes to the natural world.

To Jesse Wilkinson for giving me my very first job assisting him on wildlife camera work, which in turn helped me to become the wildlife cameraman that I am today.

I'd like to thank Christopher Bridge for taking me under his wing and teaching me more about birds in my early days of birding.

A huge thanks to the Kilchoan community and neighbours for welcoming me into the village with open arms.

I would like to thank my agents Jan Croxson, Louise Leftwich, Borra Garson and Megan Page for spotting me on telly and for believing in me when hardly anyone did.

And to Nicola Crane and the team at Octopus for making the book happen.

I would like to thank Jowita Przystał for teaching me about dance, teaching me how to be myself and for having so much patience with me!

And lastly, I would like to thank Nathan Joyce for helping me write this book.

ABOUT THE AUTHOR

Hamza Yassin is a Scottish wildlife cameraman and presenter, a skilled ornithologist and the winner of the 2022 series of *Strictly Come Dancing*.

Born in Sudan, Hamza moved to Scotland when he was young. He has a degree in Zoology with Conservation after studying at Bangor University, and a Masters in Biological Photography and Imaging from the University of Nottingham.

He made his first television appearance on *The One Show*, then went on to present the CBeebies show *Let's Go for a Walk*, in the role of Ranger Hamza. He featured in a book based on the series, which won the Sainsbury's Children's Book Prize for Best Activity Book 2021.

Since then, Hamza has appeared on *This Morning*, *Countryfile*, *Animal Park* and in the David Attenborough documentary, *Wild Isles*.

Hamza has also presented his own Channel 4 documentaries, *Scotland: My Life in the Wild* and *Scotland: Escape to the Wilderness*, and was the podcast host of the second series of *Get Birding*. In September 2023 he also presented the BBC documentary *Hamza Yassin's Birds of Prey*.

© hamzayassin90
🐦 HamzaYassin3